How to EN JOY LIVING

By James A. Nelson

How to Handle Life's Hurts
How to Enjoy Living

Dr. James A. Nelson

How to EN JOY LIVING

ACCENT BOOKS
Denver, Colorado

ACCENT BOOKS

A division of Accent Publications, Inc.
12100 W. Sixth Avenue
P.O. Box 15337
Denver, Colorado 80215

Copyright©1982 Accent Publications, Inc.
Printed in the United States of America

Library of Congress Catalog Card Number 82-70774

ISBN 0-89636-087-3

I gratefully dedicate this book to the members and friends of Trinity Baptist Church, Santa Barbara, California, whose support and encouragement have been indispensable factors in my ministry among them.

Contents

Preface

Life is meant to be enjoyed. Your life is included. Don't let anyone or anything take this conviction away from you. Not even your religion. Especially not your religion! Our religion should expand the fact that God wants us to enjoy living.

It's no exaggeration to say that God enjoys the eternal life He's living. He always has and always will. Since we are made in His image—men and women, young and old—we also are to relish life, use it, share it. Job 38:6,7 speaks of the residents of heaven shouting for joy, and of the stars and planets singing. Jesus said that He wants His followers to allow His joy to fill their lives (John 15:11). Our Heavenly Father's enjoyment of life peaks when one outside his family becomes a member of His family by faith in His Son, the Saviour of the world (Luke 15:7,10).

So it shouldn't surprise us that we, being made in God's likeness, should have within us the desire to enjoy living. But life is to be enjoyed in a responsible manner. We must utilize life properly, not in a mad, panting pursuit of selfish pleasure technically called hedonism, but in a way that shares His delight positively with others by using it to build them up.

As the Bible talks about the people who walk across its pages, it often points out their finest hours, times when life was most rewarding. By seeing how their lives became so enjoyable, we too can touch such heights.

We'll trace the course these people trod in reaching rich days. We'll learn how life is to be lived so it fulfills, just as the Designer intended. So, let these pages lift you up to many a fine hour. Here's to truly great living!

James A. Nelson

This book and your Bible . . .

I want to share a fear with you. I fear that you will go through this book without taking the time to read the Scripture references in your Bible. True, without turning to the passages and thinking through what you read, you will complete the book more quickly. But it will be at serious cost, for you will not begin to receive all we have prayerfully intended for you. Savor God's Word. Ask the Holy Spirit to speak to you personally through it.

In the writing of this book, one of two methods could have been employed. All the Scripture references might have been written out in full where they occur in the course of the writing. Doing this would have extended the pages of this book beyond reason, and it might have made the reader a bit lazy. The second option was to count on you, the reader, to refer directly to your Bible when necessary. This is the method we have chosen.

So, dispel my fear! Make the Word of God and this little volume companions. God bless, enlighten and help you as you read them both.

James A. Nelson

Chapter 1

By Being Brave
in Faith

Enjoy Living . . .
By Being Brave in Faith

Have you ever heard someone whose residence is elsewhere say, "I'd never live in Southern California! Not even if you gave it to me! Too many people. A lot of weird ones. Polluted air. And those winter mud slides! Earthquakes and forest fires. Live there? No sir! Not me!"

Having listened to this, I sometimes must point out rather sheepishly that I live in this part of the Golden State. In fact, since my wife and I have made our home in Santa Barbara, some terrifyingly destructive fires have raged in the mountains which form the city's background. We've housed scores of people in our church who have fled from these blazing infernos. Hal and Mary were one such couple. Warmly generous, it might seem as if they had never had any major setbacks in life. If you asked Hal how everything was going, his reply would most likely be, "Great, just great." Mary would smile graciously and have a word of encouragement or concern for someone.

But one awful day fire raced down the hills of our city in great leaping sheets of flame. Before it was extinguished, over two hundred homes had been destroyed and millions of dollars had gone up in smoke. One of the last houses lost belonged to Hal and Mary. Nothing was saved but the clothes they were wearing. The fireplace stood alone, scorched and naked against the sky.

The news media soon arrived, spreading cameras, cables and personnel throughout the area. One reporter held his microphone out to Mary and asked what she was feeling. Before the whirring cameras, Mary expressed her faith toward God and His purposes in everything a Christian experiences. I listened and wondered at the trust of Hal and Mary. Then we stood in the charred rubble, joined hands and prayed.

In the days which followed the devastating blaze, Hal and Mary had to draw up a list of things in the house that had been destroyed. But I've come to the conclusion that, whatever was on that report, nothing was more valuable than their faith in the Lord.

If you were to list your possessions, would unwavering trust in the Lord be found there? The essence of living is in knowing our Heavenly Father personally and trusting Him fully. Brave faith is indispensable to truly enjoying life.

As God explains in the Bible, faith is accepting as true what He has revealed in Scripture, then acting upon it, using it as a basis for daily living. Every proposition and promise God puts forward is fact and life is molded by it. Of course, this means that the Lord is viewed as a living, loving, wise, divine Person and brought into the life in a vital, permanent relationship.

Faith is not a leap in the dark. It is confidence in holy truth and the Lord God Almighty who gave it. Human beings are created with the capacity and longing to exercise this trust. Life falls short of satisfaction and fulfillment if faith is absent. We must confront the Lord and Holy Scripture in their total reliability and unquestionable truth.

In essence, true faith is brave for it is the recognition of a need beyond what one is able to supply from one's own resources. There is courage as well as humility in saying, "I need help. Specifically, I need God's help. I can't see Him with my eyes but I know He lives and cares about me. So I will come to Him, tell Him about it, and rest in Him." Hebrews 11:1,2 informs us: "Now faith is the substance of things hoped for, the evidence of things not seen. For by it the elders obtained a good report." Following this statement, we are introduced to some of the great men of the faith.

Both the Old and New Testaments urge their readers to embrace a brave trust in God. This is generally accomplished in Scripture by setting forth examples of people who gave their faith expression, or people who failed to trust God and reaped sad consequences. Putting brave faith in the Lord, the nation Israel moved mightily out of Egypt and slavery, but this initial trust didn't last. If only Israel had kept on trusting God courageously how different that people's history would have been! For a full life, it is necessary to have bold faith.

Moses, the man who led the Jews in their awesome exit from bondage, had courage to trust God when the odds were against him. He identified himself with the slave people of Israel rather than the easier, more attractive way as one of Egypt's royalty. The author of Hebrews attributes Moses' ability to do this to his faith in God and knowledge of God's will (Hebrews 11:24-28).

As we go through life, there will be times when we know the position the Lord wants us to take. It may not be popular and it may seem foolish. If we are wise, we will trust God and move in the right direction. Through this obedience, adventure and satisfaction will come to our lives. Are you at this point right now? The choice you make will change the course of your history. It will either cause you to admire yourself, or at a later time, despise yourself.

Abraham is another Old Testament figure whose life exemplifies brave faith. He chose to believe through circumstances which seemed impossibilities—like his wife's having a son in her old age. But God had promised it and Abraham believed it (Romans 4:19-22).

Because of Abraham's supreme faith, rooted in trust, he was declared righteous by the Lord and was established as the primary example of how to become a child of God (see Romans 4:11). Perhaps you are facing very significant decisions. It's time to determine what God's way is and to trust Him to guide you to a successful conclusion.

In the New Testament the Apostle Paul shows that courageous faith in the reliable Son of God is a key to contentment in life. It is difficult to project ourselves into the hard, demanding circumstances with which Paul was surrounded. He was thirsty, hungry, beaten, stoned, viciously opposed in his life calling, repeatedly put in jail (see II Corinthians 11:23-29). But he had adopted a working philosophy built on brave faith which served him well in every adversity. It can also be particularly difficult to let brave faith reign during our successes, but Paul accomplished this too. He said, "For I have learned, in whatsoever state I am, therewith to be content. I know both how to be abased, and I know how to abound: every where and in all things I am instructed both to be full and to be hungry, both to abound and to suffer need. I can do all things through Christ which strengtheneth me" (Philippians 4:11-13).

Life cannot be enjoyed without such contentment. Very few of us make our way through life without encountering some formidable obstacles which threaten to drain off all happiness. It is not an exaggeration to say that regardless of the difficulties confronting us, our cup *can* run over when we live by brave faith.

Jesus Christ is our supreme example of brave faith and a meaningful life. In the Garden of Gethsemane, Jesus sweat blood while death stalked Him (Luke 22:42-44). He wanted to escape it as much as we would. But beyond His personal desires He saw the supreme value of God's will, whatever it might require. When He prayed, "Not my will, but thine, be done" (verse 42), He meant it, even to the point of dying for the sins of the world. And He did it. Every child of God owes his place in the heavenly family to that act. But Christ couldn't have done it without very brave faith in the person, love and perfect wisdom of the Heavenly Father.

Often we say, "You do what you have to do." This is just what a mature, responsible human being does, but for a Christian there is an added factor. He does what he has to do in concert with faith in God. This makes the decision-making process more effective and brings enjoyment to life in spite of difficult decisions.

These personalities whom we have examined are great people. No Christian disputes that fact, but maybe that's part of our trouble. Their faith seems beyond us. Perhaps *they* could do it but our stature is shorter. They achieved but we can't. We're in different categories, we think.

Let's look at someone more in the nature of an average person. She is not mentioned in the faith chapter of the Bible; however, the New Testament records an episode from her life where she displays active faith.

John 12:1-8 mentions an incident involving Mary of Bethany. Mary was not an aggressive person. Her sister, Martha, had the distinction of being the leader in their family. Nor was Mary the most well-known person in the family unit. Her brother, Lazarus, was a celebrity because Christ had raised him from the dead. (That miracle caused quite a stir in Jerusalem and was probably a significant factor in Jesus' arrest and death.) One might say Mary was an ordinary "Jane Doe," devoted follower of Jesus of Nazareth much like most of us. It is this ordinariness which makes her simple demonstration of faith stimulating to those who thoughtfully read about her. If she could do it, we too are capable of such faith.

Mary entered a room where a special dinner was being served with Jesus as honored guest. Taking about a pint of costly perfume, she emptied it on His feet, then wiped those feet with her hair.

John the Apostle, who attended this celebration in Jesus' honor, was impressed with Mary for what she had done. So he recorded the incident in his Gospel as significant. Mary's act of faith registered her confidence in Christ's mission on earth. She understood what the apostles had not yet grasped. Jesus was the Messiah who would die for the sins of the world before His kingdom was set up. The Saviour recognized this, saying, "Let her alone: against the day of my burying hath she kept this" (John 12:7).

Mary's motivation for her brave, public faith was rooted in the woman's gratitude for Christ's consistent, unwearying ministries on behalf of herself and her family. A deep spiritual love had developed for Him. The absolute worthiness of His person was now in clear focus. She would be committed to Him without reservation. When any child of the Lord grasps these realities, too, motivation to a great faith is that person's possession.

The bravery in Mary's act of faith lies in her willingness to publicly profess her total allegiance to the Saviour. She was careless as to what people thought of her when it came to this issue. According to Jewish culture a Hebrew woman never unbound her hair in public. To do so was a mark of one loose in morals. See Numbers 5:11-31, especially verse 18. Realizing some might misunderstand and misjudge her motives, Mary chose to express her faith anyway. Choosing to use a precious perfume valued at a year's workingman's wages, she declared her trust. And misunderstood she was.

Is it possible that much of the lack of life-satisfaction and achievement we feel is because we are unwilling to be bold, brave and open Christians? There is little doubt of the cost. But the price we pay by hiding is higher. The basis for brave faith is a thankful love for the Son of God which grows with each day's walk with Him. As life's uncertainties and complexities which would normally empty your cup are met, true joy will flow your way when you bravely believe.

Chapter 2

By Majoring on
the Positive

Enjoy Living . . .
By Majoring on the Positive

Undoubtedly mid-life crisis has been around for a long time, but today the experience is more clearly identified. Labeling the experience helps us cope with it better. "Mid-life crisis" describes a condition in men, husbands most specifically. The age span varies with the number of people who have studied the phenomenon, but generally the crisis occurs between thirty-five and forty-five. It seems to occur during a man's drive toward prominence and achievement in his chosen field of work, at that time in a man's life when he goes for his goals with all he's got. Often it is at the expense of family considerations. Those nearest the fellow often suffer most. Sadly, he often rationalizes his involvement by telling himself it's for his family—their status, their security, a college education for the kids, a house of which his wife can be proud.

Perhaps this is true, but something else is going on, too. This husband-father, or just husband, is taking a long, intense look at himself. What he sees may deeply disturb him. He begins to wake up as to who he is and where he is in his life ambitions. The result may be panic to some significant degree. The self-assured achiever begins to waver and wonder.

In mid-life crisis it suddenly dawns on the victim that he's getting older. Something's happened to that svelt, steel-hard abdomen. He can now "pinch an inch." His body isn't what it once was when he was twenty-four. His son or daughter takes a set of tennis from him almost at will. This can't be! After all, he taught that child the game! All this can be quite depressing.

When he seriously analyzes his work he may find he's really not attaining those goals he has set. It isn't that he hasn't tried. There are just a certain number of places at the top. When they're filled, that's all. After years of working, he may realize he has risen about as high on the corporate ladder as he can.

Our American culture measures success by being the boss. Or famous, with "clout." Or earning a big salary. Or driving a sports car with a sunroof, preferably made in Italy, Germany or Japan. Or owning a rambling house on a prestigious street. When all this doesn't come together, a man is ripe for mid-life crisis. What a shame he can't learn what Jesus meant when He said, "A man's life consisteth not in the abundance of the things which he posses-seth" (Luke 12:15b).

Our American culture also worships youth, and it's evident that when thirty-five to forty-five comes, one is not young anymore. The illogical conclusion is that hope for a great life is gone. The person will just have to struggle through the rest of his days as best he can. What a man in this predicament needs to realize is that all this brainwashing about the wonders of being young is just so much deception. The most rewarding days of life are yet to be. A Bible-rooted Christian faith can be of inestimable assistance in dealing with the insecurities mid-life crisis can bring. Let's look at this bright promise of hope.

To some degree, the men of Scripture must also have wrestled with mid-life crisis. They weren't super-people, a cut above the rest of us in strength. Their sensual buds were as keen as ours. Competition, ambition and stress characterized their lives too. Some fell victim to the blows. Others discovered that out of these circumstances could come their finest hours.

In the Book of Acts a man named Philip is mentioned. We do not know his vocation, but we do know that he was part of the Christian group in Jerusalem during the early years of the first century A.D. His personal experience, as related in the Bible, would have occurred during the mid-life crisis years. He was a Jew who spoke Greek and was prominent in that sector of the church in Jerusalem where worship was conducted in the Greek language. Philip was an Israeli with an added dimension: he not only knew Hebrew culture but was exposed to the Greek world with its philosophies and cultural uniqueness. Blessed with these advantages he still remained staunchly true to the Lord.

Here was a remarkably fine man. When there was disagreement among Christians in Jerusalem, Philip was one of six chosen to settle the bickering and restore the group to harmony. He was respected and trusted for judgment and abilities. As a dedicated follower and learner of Jesus Christ, he bore the designation of disciple. Philip was so highly regarded in this capacity that he was second only to the well-known and talented first Christian martyr, Stephen (Acts 6:1-6).

Certain qualities of Philip's life are singled out in the narrative. Acts 6:3 says, "Wherefore, brethren, look ye out among you seven men of honest report, full of the Holy Ghost and wisdom, whom we may appoint over this business." It is clear this man had a good reputation. People who knew him spoke well of his person and integrity. He was a consistent believer in Jesus with a reliable testimony both in word and deed. Philip knew Christ was his Saviour and let the Holy Spirit control his daily living. Philip was stamped with the first century equivalent of a spiritual Good Housekeeping Seal of Approval.

In spite of Philip's many attributes, he was not arrogant or proud. To the contrary, he had a serving spirit. He fit right in. He was able to work with others.

Philip was willing to wait on tables. And he did (Acts 6:1-6). He cared genuinely about all the needs of the Christian group and was concerned about the unity of the people. Philip was a humble, involved Christian, diligent and responsible in what he was asked to do for the Lord and the church.

At the height of Philip's influence for God in Jerusalem, things took a bitter turn. His friend, Stephen, had been very outspoken. Angry religionists stoned Stephen to death and set out to persecute and destroy men like Philip. He became a refugee to Samaria. Driven from his home, vocation and church, he had to start life over again. Acts 8:1-5 recounts the saga.

"And Saul was consenting unto his [Stephen's] death. And at that time there was a great persecution against the church which was at Jerusalem; and they were all scattered abroad throughout the regions of Judea and Samaria, except the apostles. And devout men carried Stephen to his burial, and made great lamentation over him. As for Saul, he made havock of the church, entering into every house, and haling men and women committed them to prison. Therefore they that were scattered abroad went every where preaching the word. Then Philip went down to the city of Samaria, and preached Christ unto them."

A hard-working man in his vocation, Philip had met the increasing demands of the church. A chief spokesman in the church, Philip could have felt his life was destroyed when he fled to Samaria. But it was at this point in his life that Philip reached his finest hours. He accepted the unexpected turn of events and developed another satisfying and successful life. He didn't throw in the towel or become angry with God.

The reason for Philip's mid-life victory instead of disaster was his immediate response of total obedience to the guidance and will of the Lord as he knew it. He lived on that basis. He was God's man whatever the situation and did what the Lord wanted done. In Philip's mind, God made no mistakes. You can imagine how this conviction can alleviate mid-life crisis. If you believe you are where you are through God's love and wisdom, that He has a perfect purpose for you, that He can give you strength, that good days still lie ahead; then you can handle mid-life crisis.

Philip really meant it when he made himself available to the Lord for His purposes. He didn't just sing about commitment in church and forget it when he went out the door to face mid-life experiences. This is how the action unfolds in Acts 8:26-30.

"And the angel of the Lord spake unto Philip, saying, Arise, and go toward the south unto the way that goeth down from Jerusalem unto Gaza, which is desert. And he arose and went: and, behold, a man of Ethiopia, an eunuch of great authority under Candace queen of the Ethiopians, who had the charge of all her treasure, and had come to Jerusalem for to worship, was returning, and sitting in his chariot read Esaias the prophet. Then the Spirit said unto Philip, Go near, and join thyself to this chariot. And Philip ran thither to him, and heard him read the prophet Esaias, and said, Understandest thou what thou readest?"

It is apparent Philip followed God's desire in its broad dimension. What God asked of Philip involved danger, loneliness and difficulty. The part of Israel to which he was directed wasn't congenial to humans. And it may have been hard for Philip to leave budding success for something he knew nothing about. Today, God's Word gives the broad direction as to how we are to live. It shows us true values, presents changeless principles. Though carrying them out may not be easy, it is the way to strength in crisis. We never go wrong doing things God's way. He can save us a lot of misery and regret.

As Philip started out in the Lord's direction, he began to see the details of God's plan. He realized his experiences, training, and background had fitted him to be just the person God needed.

Acts 8:36-38 continues the narrative. "And as they went on their way, they came unto a certain water: and the eunuch said, See, here is water; what doth hinder me to be baptized? And Philip said, If thou believest with all thine heart, thou mayest. And he answered and said, I believe that Jesus Christ is the Son of God. And he commanded the chariot to stand still: and they went down both into the water, both Philip and the eunuch; and he baptized him."

Because of the way Philip handled his experience a person met Christ. A very important and politically influential person. It isn't fanciful to say that someone may meet Jesus as Saviour and be eternally in heaven because you were strong in mid-life trial and pressure. That person might be someone very dear to you. A wife. A husband. A child. A parent. But the success goes beyond the eunuch's salvation. Because of Philip, the continent of Africa was opened to the story of God's love in Christ.

Catch the vision in your situation. Your victory may touch the entire office where you work. Or a significant part of your neighborhood. Or a group of your friends. Pray big! Follow the Lord! Expect larger successes. Don't sell yourself short or settle for anything less than the whole, unique world in which you move.

Another exciting result of Philip's desire to allow God full control in his life is that Philip grew in his special capacities as a person. Twenty years after the story in Acts 8, we discover him being known as "the evangelist." Not just an evangelist. Or one of the evangelists. But *the* outstanding person in that calling. Acts 21:7,8 says: "And when we had finished our course from Tyre, we came to Ptolemais, and saluted the brethren, and abode with them one day. And the next day we that were of Paul's company departed, and came unto Caesarea: and we entered into the house of Philip the evangelist, which was one of the seven; and abode with him."

Gifts we possess develop within us as we respond to God's guidance and use them. They're like muscles: let the difficulties exert pressure against them and they get stronger. With the Lord's help, fight that first mid-life crisis successfully and you'll be more able to overcome others as they occur.

One of the most wonderful consequences of Philip's devotion was what his attitude and actions did for his family. They caught his spirit. This is what the Bible says about his daughters in Acts 21:9. "And the same man [Philip] had four daughters, virgins, which did prophesy."

Tradition tells us all four of these girls lived to old age. They became esteemed informants on early Judean Christianity. They lived for and served the Lord.

The people we want to help the most are those we love most. That's probably our family. How you meet your mid-life experiences may fashion your family's personalities. Let your experiences destroy you and you might destroy those you love. Many alcoholics are children of alcoholics. And a great percentage of divorced people are themselves from broken homes. On the other hand, letting the crisis bring about your finest hour may inspire the members of your family to great lives.

The verses incorporated here from the Book of Acts have had much to say about the Holy Spirit, the Spirit of God. He plays a central role in God's leading a life dynamically, courageously and victoriously. We must identify Him and His ways.

He is deity, as much divine as the Heavenly Father, and as much a person, too. More than just a healthy influence, He is an individual. The Bible leaves no doubt about this. So in mid-life crisis, and at all other times, Christians are dealing with a holy Person who relates Himself to them in perfect wisdom, the wisdom deity alone possesses.

One of the Spirit's particular functions is to lead the children of God. Members of the heavenly family are to be guided by Him. When we go off on our own, we walk an uncertain and potentially disappointing road.

The Holy Spirit is shown leading His followers on a world-influencing scale in Acts 13:2-4: "As they ministered to the Lord, and fasted, the Holy Ghost said, Separate me Barnabas and Saul for the work whereunto I have called them. And when they had fasted and prayed, and laid their hands on them, they sent them away." So when you ask Him for wisdom and sensitive guidance in a mid-life crisis or any situation, you don't disturb Him. Nor do you catch Him unprepared to help.

The Spirit of God lives in every Christian. The Bible puts it like this:

"What? know ye not that your body is the temple of the Holy Ghost which is in you, which ye have of God, and ye are not your own? For ye are bought with a price: therefore glorify God in your body, and in your spirit, which are God's" (I Corinthians 6:19,20).

The Spirit is right inside our soul, available at a moment's notice. We don't need to shout for Him to hear us. The Holy Spirit is also within the church in a very special way. He is there as a real, inseparable part of every group of real Christians. Paul reminded the church in Corinth of this: "Know ye not that ye are the temple of God, and that the Spirit of God dwelleth in you? If any man defile the temple of God, him shall God destroy; for the temple of God is holy, which temple ye are" (I Corinthians 3:16,17).

The church where Christ is honored, where the Bible is the text, and where people love each other is a viable avenue of help for Christians in mid-life crisis. For maximum aid in dealing with crisis, you need to be part of a church body. Agreed, all churches have faults and flaws because imperfect people are there. But it's the special place God has seen fit to inhabit by the Holy Spirit. We must not neglect the church.

As we read the Bible and watch the Holy Spirit in action, we find He functions with three thoughts in mind: absolute truth, Christ's exaltation, and genuine love. Truth means that which is the opposite of falsehood or deception. Wherever genuine truth is found, the Holy Spirit has an instrument to use for our help. This is why we must be truthful in relating to Him, honestly coming to Him as we are.

Truth also defines Scripture. In all He does, the Spirit of God will not act outside the Word of God. He will never depart from its principles. This keeps us from fooling ourselves about solving mid-life crises in a somewhat questionable way. No exceptions! He's the Spirit of Truth.

"Even the Spirit of truth; whom the world cannot receive, because it seeth him not, neither knoweth him: but ye know him; for he dwelleth with you, and shall be in you" (John 14:17). "Ye have not chosen me, but I have chosen you, and ordained you, that ye should go and bring forth fruit, and that your fruit should remain: that whatsoever ye shall ask of the Father in my name, he may give it you" (John 15:16).

"Howbeit when he, the Spirit of truth, is come, he will guide you into all truth: for he shall not speak of himself; but whatsoever he shall hear, that shall he speak: and he will shew you things to come" (John 16:13).

The supreme objective of the Holy Spirit is to exalt Christ. His ministry is built upon the person of the Lord Jesus. When we are troubled, it is Jesus whom the Holy Spirit makes real. He helps us by means of our crisis to honor Christ and bring Him glory. This keeps us from destructive pride in our successes. The acid test of the active presence of the Holy Spirit, as opposed to false spirits, is His making Jesus supreme. Without the Son of God we flounder. Hear Christ make the statement Himself: "He shall glorify me: for he shall receive of mine, and shall shew it unto you" (John 16:14).

We can always count on the Holy Spirit to function in the attitude of divine love. Never in harshness. Never pridefully. Never selfishly. Never vengefully or vindictively. As Scripture puts it, "But the fruit of the Spirit is love" (Galatians 5:22a). In mid-life turmoil you needn't fear that the Spirit will berate you. In love, He will aid you. With love you will be enabled to live through the experience. Through your witness you will be exerting the greatest influence in human comprehension.

Chapter 3

By Being Committed to Love

Enjoy Living . . .
By Being Committed to Love

We live in uncertain times. Many people in our towns today are afraid to take a walk after dark. Muggers and rapists are prevalent in hamlets, and New Yorkers shun Central Park even in broad daylight for the same reason. Respect for person, property and law seems to be rapidly fading.

"Perfect" marriages are breaking up, sometimes after thirty or forty years. Kids from the "finest" families are hooked on drugs. Premarital sex is somewhat taken for granted by an increasing number of people.

At work an employee gets a substantial raise. His family celebrates—until the new paycheck is brought home and he finds he has less than before because the raise nudged him into a higher tax bracket. More means less.

Government seems to get bigger continually. Every four years fresh new planks are built into party platforms. The promises sound great and we believe there's hope after all. The new wood smells good. But the promises seem to disappear like mist and disillusionment sets in.

So you dash off to church to get a comforting word from God and a bit of guidance for solving the puzzle of life. But some well-educated clergyman of whom you stand in awe tells you the Lord hasn't spoken through the Bible after all. The minister suggests you don't need His advice anyway. You've got what's necessary for happiness inside you. Just bring it out. You wonder, "Doesn't the minister know how confused and empty I am?" And, unhelped, you return home.

Whatever our situation, wherever we may be, the most extreme conditions cannot keep us from joyous living if we walk with God. Surely we will have our low moments. Life gets pretty real, as the saying goes, and being a Christian doesn't exempt one from realities. But God wants to lift us above the realities to great heights of living.

The Bible's narrative shows that often great moments come during difficult times. The Book of Judges covers an era during which everything had come apart at the seams. Judges 17:6 describes just how bad the times were: "Every man did that which was right in his own eyes." Now, that's pretty frightening. Stop and think a moment. Can you imagine what your town would be like if that were true today?

During this period, a woman lived who is a great example of triumphing over hard times. In addition to experiencing history out of control, she had some weighty personal problems. A young Israeli had moved to her country of Moab. He and she met and were married. The Jew's name, Mahlon, means "sickly." At some point in their marriage, Mr. Sickly died. Such an experience is never easy for a wife. Then his brother, Chilion, expired. The woman's father-in-law also died, leaving his wife, Naomi, scratching to stay alive. Finally, a sad and shattered woman, Naomi decided to return to Israel. Her long-suffering daughter-in-law, Ruth, accompanied her.

A book of the Bible bears Ruth's name. Of the sixty-six books in Scripture, only two are named for their heroine. (The other is Esther.) The name, Ruth, means "friendly." Perhaps the people of Moab were like the Hebrews who weren't quick to name their children. They waited awhile, observed the personality of the child, then named him or her accordingly. Ruth must have been a cooing, cuddly, amicable baby girl.

Ruth became very significant in the plan of God. She was the great grandmother of David, the king, the man who would be held in highest regard by Jewish people, even today. Beyond this, however, she was an ancestress of Jesus Christ (Matthew 1:5). So it might be helpful to know what her finest hour was. If you know the biography of Ruth, it won't surprise you that when she gave herself to a personal ministry of companionship with her mother-in-law Naomi, Ruth began to live some of the finer moments of her life. Ruth 1:14-16 describes the occasion:

"And they lifted up their voice, and wept again: and Orpah kissed her mother in law; but Ruth clave unto her. And she [Naomi] said, Behold, thy sister in law is gone back unto her people, and unto her gods: return thou after thy sister in law. And Ruth said, Intreat me not to leave thee, or to return from following after thee: for whither thou goest, I will go; and where thou lodgest, I will lodge: thy people shall be my people, and thy God my God."

Ruth became Naomi's friend in the fullest sense of the word and through the service of true friendship entered into a fuller life herself. It is not recorded that Ruth had any special gifts or capabilities, that she was equipped to do anything outstanding as we would evaluate it. But she could be a close and helpful companion. She could fill a void in her mother-in-law's life. She could strengthen and encourage in difficult times.

For us as well as Ruth, this can be one of life's finest hours. And it's something everyone can do. People around us are crying for someone to reach out to them like this. Charles M. Schulz's book, *I Need All the Friends I Can Get,* is a series of cartoon panels depicting our friend, Charlie Brown, as a fellow who needs a companion. People and circumstances have made him the person on the outside looking in. He says, "Nobody likes me . . . nobody cares if I live or die." Does the thought seem familiar? Perhaps Naomi felt the same way. Maybe you have, too.

In the cartoon, Lucy, Charlie's persistent antagonist, challenges him to define a friend. Charlie Brown suggests, "A friend is someone you can sock on the arm." Or in reference to tennis: "A friend is someone who will take the side with the sun in his eyes." Most of us can relate to, "A friend is someone who likes you even when the other guys are around." Charlie's pal, Pigpen, suggests, "A friend is someone who accepts you for what you are." Naomi might have said, "A friend is Ruth."

In reading the story of Ruth, we wonder what her attitude was toward her mother-in-law. Undoubtedly, Ruth felt a sense of responsibility for Naomi. Naomi was devastated. The hand of death had rested heavily upon her family. She was growing older and when she needed security most, it was slipping away from her and she was helpless to stop it. She probably felt a sense of aloneness, as if she had been forsaken by the Lord.

Ruth could not deny there was a need. And she could meet it. Accepting that responsibility may not have been easy. A lot of grace, understanding and determination were required of Ruth. And she stepped forward in that spirit to meet the need.

Can you think of people who are 20th Century Naomis? The moment you respond as Ruth did you'll begin to enjoy life. Maybe in a self-centered world this doesn't make sense, but in God's kingdom it's pure wisdom. We think about ourselves and our circumstances too much. Maybe what we ought to do is focus on people whose condition is far worse than ours, and reach out to minister to them by companionship. We're responsible for each other.

Ruth recognized the fact that being Naomi's companion was an opportunity for Ruth's growth and development as a person. Ruth promised, "Thy God shall be my God." Knowing the Lord comes from doing what the Lord would do if He stood in our shoes. No one can minister like Ruth did without developing a deeper relationship with God and discovering things about Him which couldn't be grasped any other way.

Should your opportunity to befriend be with an older individual, as Ruth's was, it is entirely possible he or she will add to your knowledge of living. That brings an enrichment of life you can't get from books; only living long brings it. Older people who have gone through rough waters have wisdom as to how to navigate the waves. There is no need for us to learn from hard and debilitating experience what they can teach us in a short time. Do you see how deeply everyone is benefited by this ministry of companionship?

Ruth found a full life by earnest, intense commitment to Naomi. She locked herself into the woman's life. She vowed to be with her in all circumstances. "Where you go I will go; your people will be my people; I'll live where you live, whatever the surroundings. I'll die with you" (paraphrase). There are such deep, meaningful implications, it is little wonder the words are quoted by many brides and grooms as part of their wedding vows.

Willingness to make a commitment is rapidly diminishing in our century. Many people just don't want to get involved. The more this spirit dominates, the more life loses its luster. Because many marriages are devoid of commitment they are falling apart. At this moment are you committed to a worthy person or worthy objectives and convictions? To someone other than yourself? To something other than your own interests?

One of Ruth's attitudes which seems to absorb all others, giving them a richness, is that of an all-conquering love. She really cared about her forlorn mother-in-law. It gave her a selflessness which enabled her to put her interests second to the needs of Naomi. Boaz, Ruth's husband-to-be, recognized and greatly admired this selflessness. It is not out of line to say that such love put her into the lineage of the coming Son of God. Love tears down the highest barriers between people. It solves the harshest conflict, counteracts the saddest circumstance. The Lord can produce love in your life, and this love will build within you a fierce but warm loyalty to what is worthwhile, promoting your life to finest hours.

Perhaps the most significant thing this powerful love does is give one the spirit and mind-set of ministry. The attitude of Jesus takes hold of that person. The eternal purpose of Christ coming into our world was to serve. This marks the individual who lets Christ love through him. No longer does he demand, "Tell me my rights." Rather, he seriously requests, "Show me my responsibilities." Here is the essence of the Christian calling. And here is the road to joyful living.

The ministry of companionship opens up the door to many exciting possibilities. Friendship with the Heavenly Father is one. It's a staggering thought to realize God wants fellowship with us. Equally impressive is the fact that we have been created with the capability to be a companion to God. No other creation of God can claim this ability. Not even angels! By our faith in Christ the Saviour, barriers between God and us have been removed and we can live with Him in friendship. That's enjoying life! Adam and Eve entered into it. Abraham and Moses did too. So can you, and no door of earthly circumstance can be slammed in your face.

What about applying this same principle and privilege to companionship to Jesus? He rose from the dead. He's alive forever. He's someone we can know in wonderful companionship. The Saviour who needed the friendship of His disciples has that same longing today. We can satisfy it. The Apostle John wanted all Christians to enjoy living on this level and wrote, "Our fellowship is with the Father, and with his Son Jesus Christ" (I John 1:3b).

Do you have companionship with the other member of the sacred Trinity—the Holy Spirit? Christians must join hands with Him in a daily, close relationship if their joyful experience as children of God is to be complete. Note this plea in the well-rounded benediction prayer of Paul: "The grace of the Lord Jesus Christ, and the love of God, and the communion [fellowship] of the Holy Ghost [Spirit] be with you all" (II Corinthians 13:14).

One's home life cannot do without the ministry of companionship. Your spouse must be your dearest friend. You cannot reach fine hours within marriage if this is not so. As Christians, you and your spouse have been bound together in life's highest association. Exert yourself to make it rich. Offer yourself not only as partner and lover, but as best friend. Encourage your spouse to be that grand person he or she can be through your ministry of companionship. See that it is marked by compatibility of goals and philosophy; communication built on confidence; a concert of effort in making your way through life as husband and wife. Peter calls you, "heirs together of the grace of life" (I Peter 3:7). Act as though this were so, and see what such a companionship will bring.

The Book of Ruth lays down for us a lovely story. In fact Goethe said, "We have nothing so lovely in the whole range of epic and idyllic poetry." But the most beautiful fact within it is that the heights its heroine reached in her life so long ago may be realized by you in the same way centuries later. Tragedies need not stop you.

Chapter 4

By Growing a People Garden

Enjoy Living . . .
By Growing a People Garden

It all began in the Garden of Eden. Not only the history of the human family but also that family's on-going love affair with gardens. Apparently men and women are made, at least in part, for gardens. Human beings all around the world plant gardens. We seem to need the spiritual satisfaction gardening brings, as well as the food gardens give to the physical dimension of man.

There is something therapeutic about working in a garden. It's a plot with life in it. We are reminded that here decay and death are not the dominant qualities surrounding us. There is beauty in a garden. It's a good place to work and from it essential enjoyment in living can be discovered. Perhaps God had some of these things in mind when He placed Adam and Eve in a garden.

Come to think of it, a garden setting will characterize our world and universe after Jesus returns again with His saints in power and glory, taking over the rulership of planet earth. Isaiah describes that time and condition like this: "The wilderness and the solitary place shall be glad for them; and the desert shall rejoice, and blossom as the rose. It shall blossom abundantly, even with joy and singing" (Isaiah 35:1,2a).

The garden-like term, Paradise, is sometimes used to define heaven. The beauty of a garden is closely associated with heaven. To the thief who trusted Christ as he was being crucified with Jesus, the Saviour promised, "To day shalt thou be with me in paradise" (Luke 23:43b). Encouraging Christians to be strong and persistent in their stand for Him, Christ declared, "To him that overcometh will I give to eat of the tree of life, which is in the midst of the paradise of God" (Revelation 2:7). This last book of the Bible closes by expressing the beauty of a pure river and tree of life referred to in Revelation 2:7. Health for the world seems to come from the garden of heaven (Revelation 22:1-3). In II Corinthians 12:1-4, Paul makes the impressive claim that God gave him the privilege at one time of being in this magnificent environment. He claimed that though he might have desired to tell about it he couldn't find words that would ably convey the grandeur and beauty of Paradise.

At times, Scripture likens people to parts of a

garden. With reference to the blessed, happy man who finds his delight in God and His interests, David says, "He shall be like a tree planted by the rivers of water, that bringeth forth his fruit in his season; his leaf also shall not wither; and whatsoever he doeth shall prosper" (Psalm 1:3). The Lord speaks of the Jewish nation in garden vocabulary: "For the vineyard of the Lord of hosts is the house of Israel, and the men of Judah his pleasant plant" (Isaiah 5:7a). Even the coming Messiah who would bear the iniquities of the world is referred to in garden terms: "He shall grow up before him as a tender plant, and as a root out of a dry ground" (Isaiah 53:2a). When the Lord Jesus spoke of the union of Christians and Himself, He used plant terminology. One can almost feel the surging life of, "I am the vine; ye are the branches: He that abideth in me, and I in him, the same bringeth forth much fruit: for without me ye can do nothing" (John 15:5). In Scripture, the garden is an important vehicle in describing some of the highest spiritual realities.

There are many kinds of gardens. Some have plants of many varieties; others are highly specialized. Vegetable gardens are popular with many of us in these days of high food prices. The Gallup poll disclosed that thirty-four million, or forty-three percent of American households produced some or all of their vegetables in 1980. Scores of public gardens bloom across America. Someone has estimated that one of these gardens is within a day's drive of almost everyone.

But there is another kind of garden—the "people garden." This type of gardening cultivates an interest in the well-being of other people. It brings them to fullest bloom as individuals. It sees the talents others have and aids in the development of those talents. It is sensitive to the knowledge that many are withered by the lack of love in their lives. It waters them with love. It observes the person who is emotionally undernourished and feeds him the food of God's Word. The diligent gardener gains the brightest enjoyment from this type of garden. The people gardener is ever expanding, strengthening in his faith, while one who is primarily preoccupied with himself shrinks in awareness and usefulness.

How does one begin to succeed in this type of gardening? He must start with the feeling that people are important, that each has something he can contribute to life that will make the world a better place. He must realize when one person fails a bit of failure comes to us all, and when one person achieves all of us gain in some way. There is challenge in knowing that God sees everyone as worthwhile. Central to the Christian faith is the ageless, divine statement, "For God so loved the world, that he gave his only begotten Son, that whosoever believeth in him should not perish, but have everlasting life" (John 3:16). Human beings are created in the image of God, and an appreciation of this is absolutely indispensable to the people gardener.

Being a people gardener also demands a noticeable openness to others. The people gardener must be approachable. Certain things show it: a warm, genuine smile, a kind hello, a word of commendation or encouragement, an interest in others, an absence of judgmentalism or harshness. In short—the spirit of Christ in everything.

In order to be Christlike, the people gardener must also live in the garden of the Lord. He will permit the Son of God to speak to him through Scripture. He will abide in Christ to the best of his ability. He will give the Lord the right to live through his life. He will place every gift and ability at the Saviour's feet.

He will try to be Christlike in everything. He who is tended by the Master Gardener is most able to become an effective people gardener himself.

The story of Aquila and Priscilla will serve as an example of people gardening (Acts 18:24-28). This husband-wife team was dedicated to the same spiritual philosophy: absolute fidelity to the person of Christ and dedication to His cause. Their commitment was so strong that they were willing to be exiled from their home city. Wherever they lived they started a church in their home. When a couple have this much commitment, they have a firm base from which to garden. If you are contemplating marriage, remember how important this spiritual compatibility is and settle for nothing less than what Aquila and Priscilla had.

Aquila and Priscilla were business partners as well as marriage partners. They shared the business of making tents as well as people gardening. They understood each other and were a mutual support. You and your spouse may not work at the same secular employment, but you should be interested in what the other is doing. Be willing to give and take advice as you become familiar with your partner's daily task. The more this relationship is healthy, the more effective your teamwork in people gardening.

This husband and wife duo also gave each other time to be themselves. They respected the talent and capabilities each possessed. Each developed as an individual as well as a beloved and much-needed partner. This kind of respect carries over into the people gardening activity. Each realizes the other can do a special job with particular people plants and encourages him to do it. In love, let your spouse grow as a person.

The essence of this couple is that they were going in the same direction. There were no divided loyalties or disagreement as to life priorities. For the glory of God they were set to help people develop. Though they manufactured tents, they were chiefly in the people business. Do you think their home rang with the true joy of living? No doubt about it! With eyes off themselves and nerves desensitized to misunderstandings, they were able to concentrate on growing a people garden.

A man named Apollos was one of their plants. His home, Alexandria, Egypt, was respected as a learning center. It was famous around the world as a cultural center. Apollos was a solid reflection of the city. He had attained a reputation as an Old Testament scholar who understood, mastered, and expounded Scripture capably. Centuries later, Martin Luther so admired him that he considered Apollos as a strong possibility for having authored the New Testament Book of Hebrews.

With these enviable intellectual properties, Apollos was an eloquent speaker. A mind with depth and a person of speaking ability do not always go together. Evidently neither Moses nor Paul had the combination (Exodus 4:10; I Corinthians 2:1-3). But Apollos was able to communicate what he knew and do so with refinement. It is not too much to say he was the most skilled speaker in the apostolic church. His was a soul on fire with love for God, people, goodness and truth. His admirable ability was joined with an equally admirable character. But, like even the best and most talented humans, Apollos had his weaknesses, particularly a blind spot here and there in his spiritual knowledge.

Aquila and Priscilla, united in people gardening, recognized the lack, felt they could help, and so cultivated this fine man. Nowhere do we find Aquila and Priscilla acting impulsively. To the contrary, they coupled courage with love and tact. Rushing into people gardening without God's guidance can do more harm than good. This is a holy venture which requires the Lord's fullest help for success.

But once the couple knew their involvement was of God they invited Apollos into their home (Acts 18:26). They got close to him, really put forth an effort to know Apollos as a person. Though he was omitting certain factors essential to New Testament Christianity they accepted him as he was. They were not aloof or critical. Apollos was not contradicted or rejected by Aquila and Priscilla.

We cannot grow people gardens in negative soil. The plants won't develop; they'll suffocate. This doesn't mean that matters needing change should be ignored. In any kind of garden weeding is necessary, but when it is a people garden those weeds can't be yanked out with calloused hands. How we go about serious plant care is greatly important. If we don't realize this it could cut off our success almost entirely. The meekness and gentleness of Christ to which Paul refers in II Corinthians 10:1 have to be some of our most frequently used gardening tools. We must live close to the Saviour so we will be sensitive in guiding others in personal growth.

When Apollos visited, Aquila and Priscilla gave positive instruction precisely where the man needed it. It speaks well of Apollos, too, that he willingly received the aid offered in the kind way it was intended. Carefully, skillfully, accurately, Aquila and Priscilla exposed Apollos to the Word of Christ, doing their best to explain it. Being careful to let God speak, they filled in the gaps in the scholar-orator's knowledge. People don't need what we think but what the Lord has said. People gardens come into beautiful flower only when the divine Word is made the food of the mind and heart. The gardener must be an expert in spiritual nutrients and how they are applied.

The most beautiful gardens in the world are those made up of men and women who are maturing under the loving eye of responsible Christians. If we cannot be great (whatever greatness is), we can become the means of making others great. In the process, the person who grows a people garden will find life more rewarding than he ever thought possible. And his influence will be felt long after he has gone to heaven. Garden, Christian! Garden!

Chapter 5

By Doing an Errand
for God

Enjoy Living . . .
By Doing an Errand for God

For what is the town where you live noted? More than one thing, probably. Many cities across America are associated with specific landmarks. The Golden Gate Bridge is associated with San Francisco. Philadelphia is known for Independence Hall. New Orleans causes one to think of the Mardi Gras and the French Quarter. This same kind of association could be made with cities of the ancient world. Babylon was recognized for its massive walls and spectacular Hanging Gardens. Memphis, Egypt, housed fabulous palace buildings erected at substantial cost in money and human lives. Damascus, capital of today's Syria, was known as one of the world's oldest cities even millennia ago. Indeed, at the time the New Testament began, Damascus was four thousand years old. It was founded by Uz, grandson of Shem who was one of Noah's sons. You can partially understand the saying, "The world began at Damascus and will end there."

Damascus is mentioned in the earliest pages of the Bible. The city is closely associated with the history of Israel. Eliezer, chief administrator of Abraham's household and all his wealth, was from Damascus. King David conquered the city, building garrisons there to house his troops and compelling the citizens of Damascus to pay him tribute.

Elisha, great man of God, spoke prophecies about its king's recovery from deathly illness and the ultimate Syrian conquest because of cruelties to Israel. He said to the Syrian king-to-be, "I know the evil that thou wilt do unto the children of Israel: their strong holds wilt thou set on fire, and their young men wilt thou slay with the sword, and wilt dash their children, and rip up their women with child" (II Kings 8:12). Bad blood has existed between Damascus and Jerusalem for centuries. It hasn't changed today. Little wonder that Isaiah, Jeremiah and Amos prophesied against the city and the nation. "The burden of Damascus. Behold, Damascus is taken away from being a city, and it shall be a ruinous heap" (Isaiah 17:1).

But what concerns us now are the two important events which took place both outside and inside Damascus' walls during New Testament times. These happenings significantly intertwine.

One day on the great caravan road that led to the

city, and over which much wealth had passed through the centuries, something occurred that changed the history of the world. Saul of Tarsus, that fuming, fiery, ruthless persecutor of the Christian church, was riding toward Damascus. His purpose was to seize and bind all followers of Jesus. Close to the city gates he had an experience he often recounted in later days. A brilliant, blinding light from heaven struck him, throwing him from his horse to the ground. There, flat on his face in the dust of the road, he met Jesus. It turned Saul's life around completely. Physically sightless, but spiritually sighted for the first time in his life, he was led to Damascus by his associates. They found him a room on Straight Street. Saul was so stunned that he lay in that room three days without eating or drinking.

At this point, the Damascus story touches the thought being considered in this chapter. Life becomes alive, filled with joy and meaning when a person believes he has been put on earth for a reason and when he makes himself available to God to achieve His purpose. Created in God's image, men and women are put on earth to function in partnership with Him. Life's cup runs over when we understand this and will go on an errand for Him. We think that pursuing our own plans and desires will bring joy, and this may be partially true. But the fullest possible enjoyment of life is found in completing errands the Lord assigns.

Think back a bit. When you were a child wasn't it true that you felt really satisfied when you had completed an errand for Mom or Dad? They had trusted you with something and you had done the best you could. Their appreciation and your achievement brought you a full cup of enjoyment. The same holds true between you and God.

Having begun to work with Saul, the Lord called on a man whom He needed to carry out the next step in His plan for Saul. Acts 9:10-19 tells the story of Ananias' errand, one he never regretted obeying, I am sure. He was to go down to Straight Street, find Saul, encourage him by Christian love, help him regain his eyesight and baptize him into the church.

"Easy errand," you say. You think it was exciting and therefore gladly accepted. Not for a minute. This was a dangerous, disagreeable, distasteful job. There was considerable religious unrest in Damascus already. Furthermore, of all the persecutors, Saul was most feared and disliked by Christians. The thought must have run through Ananias' mind that maybe Saul was only pretending to be blind. Perhaps it was a ruse to corner even more Christians. No one would have put it past a man like Saul of Tarsus to try such deceit.

But, after expressing his concern to God, Ananias went on the errand. He carried out the Lord's desires perfectly. Because he did, you and I and myriad others have heard of the grace of God in Jesus Christ. God knew what He was doing. And in later years when Ananias looked back on his notable errand, what joy surely flooded his being! With an inward shudder he must have thought, "What if I hadn't done it?"

Certain aspects of Ananias' involvement in heaven's errand can be helpful to us as we seek to carry out God's errands in our day. Ananias was a born-again believer in the Saviour. Once Ananias began the errand, he trusted God with no thought of turning back. The Bible calls Ananias, "a certain disciple at Damascus" (Acts 9:10). Before God sent him on His errand, Ananias had done all he could to learn of Christ and His doctrine. He tried to live the way his Master would if He were in Damascus. He was truly a disciple. This is the kind of individual God can use for His special errands. Each of us must *be* before we *do*. The order cannot be reversed. The depth of our Christianity, the consistency in our study of Christ, the seriousness with which we take our Christian faith are all very important ingredients in our usefulness to God. Enjoyment of living depends greatly upon having the proper spiritual attitude.

It should encourage us to observe that as far as we know this Damascus disciple was an ordinary, private Christian in his work-a-day world. It is not recorded he was a church official—not a pastor or a deacon or a teacher. Just a respected brother pursuing a craft, vocation or profession. Perhaps he was retired! He was like the majority of us. Whether you work from nine to five, eight to four-thirty, the swing shift or the graveyard shift, or all day long like wives and mothers do, your secular duties aren't meant to keep you from God's errands. This matter of partnership with God is not meant for church professionals only. Ananias knew this. We should believe it too. If going on errands for the Lord was for a select few, how few of God's desires for the world could be accomplished. Whether pastors or people in the pew, we are brothers and sisters together in ministry. This means all of us can tap the source of a joyful life.

Consider also the point that Ananias was tuned in to God. He was on heaven's channel, so to speak. Worldly interference wasn't causing static or making the picture roll incomprehensibly. God just said one word—called his name—and Ananias said, "Yes, Lord." One cannot hear or see what God wants done if he does not live close to God's heart every day. Don't let sins build up or life's cares increasingly dominate so that the voice of the Lord calling you to an errand of importance cannot be heard. Measure what is really worth your time and energy by how well it will stand up in eternity. This doesn't mean one can have no interests other than those we call "spiritual." It merely says we must put first things first.

From the story of Ananias, we learn also that we must be completely open to where God is going and what He is doing in the "now." We can't live in what used to be, whether that was good or bad. If we are living in the past we will not be receptive to the errands He has for us in the present. As it did for Ananias, it may mean breaking down some philosophical prejudices. Can you imagine Ananias calling

Saul, the Christian-killer, "Brother Saul"? (Acts 9:17). This not only required grace; it took courage and self-discipline. We must not be frozen in old patterns of bitterness. The Word of God, the direction of the Lord must determine our course of action.

In order to be effective for the Lord, we must be allied with God's grace. We must understand that mercy is the Lord's way. Since Christ died for the sins of the world, the flood gates of divine love have been opened and heaven's grace has poured forth. Therefore, we who run on errands for God must feel as He feels toward people and situations and act with graciousness. Our mission cannot be accomplished in this age by any other method. As Ananias stood before blind Saul and spoke to him, we understand we are to reassure those to whom God sends us that Christ is living and hears the earnest pleas of all who trust Him. We are to let them know beyond a doubt that there is hope in the Son of God, that their spiritual experience is real. Christianity is no dream.

One has to be impressed with another facet of Ananias' character which made him effective in his errand. He was a man of concern. He was concerned for the honor of God and the people of the Lord. Ananias sought the highest honor for the One who sent him. He understood the demanding, serious nature of his errand and pursued it with a great devotion.

Often an errand on which we are sent will be in behalf of another Christian. We need to reflect concern in our involvements for the cause of Christ. What one does or does not do may have a serious effect upon other Christians. True ministers of Christ are characterized by a certain protectiveness of the Christian family.

Children of God who are conscientiously engaged in a task for their Heavenly Father should know it is not done without His reward. There will be a reward beyond the solid delight of enjoyment of living. Ananias discovered what people doing God's bidding have always rejoiced to find: in Christ the bitterest enemies become brothers. Walls are shattered. Fear and suspicion give way to peace and confidence. Fellowship is born where once there was estrangement. The reconciling force the human race needs emerges through completing the Lord's plan. Thus, the one who has carried out the sacred errand feels he has made a permanent contribution to the society of which he is a part.

Ananias became Saul's first Christian friend. New friendships should not be an unexpected by-product of Christianity in action. Whether or not Paul and his Christian friend from Damascus saw each other often in the following years we do not know. But a relationship was begun which eternity will serve to enrich. A wider circle of new friends results from doing errands for God.

As Ananias heard about his friend Paul in the man's later, widespread ministries, he probably was grateful for the privilege of having had a lasting influence on the preacher from Tarsus. Ananias first called Paul "brother," but the term became Paul's own precious designation for himself, describing how he felt toward fellow believers. It was Ananias who invested that word with meaning for Paul. The Apostle, who made grace and graciousness the kingpin of his theology, saw it demonstrated first in Ananias—before he ever learned the doctrine of God's grace from the Holy Spirit. Much of what Paul became can be traced back to his friend who went on an errand for God. Nothing is greater than influencing a life toward permanent good. Errand people do just that. This too is your reward.

Chapter 6

By Commitment to
Something Worthwhile

Enjoy Living . . .
By Commitment to Something Worthwhile

God's Word is replete with questions. The first question in the Bible is sobering in its implications. Walking through the Garden of Eden, the Lord called out to Adam, "Where art thou?" (Genesis 3:9). He may be asking us the same question. We should seriously consider it. Where are we spiritually and morally? Are our priorities in order? With reference to youth, the psalmist asked, "Wherewithal shall a young man cleanse his way? By taking heed thereto according to thy word" (Psalm 119:9). Yes, this Scripture is important to people of all ages.

In the New Testament, Jesus asks a deeply probing, double-pronged question: "For what is a man profited, if he shall gain the whole world, and lose his own soul? Or what shall a man give in exchange for his soul?" (Matthew 16:26). In light of Christ's questions, society's materialistic philosophy doesn't make a lot of sense. The author of Hebrews asks, "How shall we escape, if we neglect so great salvation; which at the first began to be spoken by the Lord, and was confirmed unto us by them that heard him . . . ?" (Hebrews 2:3). Projecting ourselves into eternity, we conclude that no earthly thing is worth making us oblivious to God's love in Jesus Christ. In fact, our enjoyment of life today is tied to our personal concern with the salvation of others. As Christians, we must not ignore the evangelistic imperative, for these words apply to us too. We must care whether or not people in our towns and around the world know Christ as Saviour.

What matters most to you? Your life is probably being molded by your answer. Your reply shows where you really are in the business of living.

Your cup of joyous living can never run over without commitment to something worthwhile. Animals may be contented without conscious dedication to an ideal, but human beings are not. We need much more from life than a satisfying response to basic physical desires. This Christian principle flies directly in the face of the constant sensual enticements to "Try me and you'll be happy"; "Get rid of those brown age spots"; "Be sexy"; "Drink my brand of beer and smoke these very low tar cigarettes"; "Drive this car"; "Enjoyment can be yours." If you've tried these things, you know that a momentary pleasure may be experienced, but without a more substantial commitment, life is still dry.

Commitment is a serious belief in a concept or person to the extent that it becomes a motivation to the way we live. Paul's words to the Ephesians describe commitment beautifully. He prays, "That Christ may dwell in your hearts by faith; that ye, being rooted and grounded in love, may be able to comprehend with all saints what is the breadth, and length, and depth, and height; and to know the love of Christ, which passeth knowledge, that ye might be filled with all the fullness of God" (Ephesians 3:17-19).

From these verses, three words suggest that there are dimensions to commitment: *Dwell,* meaning to be fully at home and welcome to every room of the house; *rooted,* which inspires a picture of a great tree sinking its roots deeply into the soil which nourishes it; and *grounded,* or built solidly upon a foundation mingling what one is with all the solid base is. Commitment is the guidance system for the ship of one's life. It must be functioning to bring enjoyment to the individual. Otherwise, life breaks up on the rocks.

Lack of commitment manifests itself in aimlessness. Sadly, this accurately describes many people. Lack of direction and goals leads one to drift along, going nowhere. There is no control; random wandering occurs.

It is possible to be committed to someone or something, yet be guilty of misusing our commitment if the object of our commitment is inferior. Much that calls for our dedication is not worthy. If we are not enriched by the commitment, it is not worthy of our time. If a commitment destroys other people or is unlikely to please and honor God; if it is tied to time and cannot relate to eternity, it is probably safe to say it is unworthy of our commitment.

Joshua is an Old Testament character whose life-style showed worthwhile commitments. The particular phase of his life which interests us is chronicled in Joshua 24:14,15: "Now therefore fear the Lord, and serve him in sincerity and in truth: and put away the gods which your fathers served on the other side of the flood, and in Egypt; and serve ye the Lord. And if it seem evil unto you to serve the Lord, choose you this day whom ye will serve; whether the gods which your fathers served that were on the other side of the flood, or the gods of the Amorites, in whose land ye dwell: but as for me and my house, we will serve the Lord."

Joshua was a name frequently given to Jewish boys. It means, "Jehovah saves." The Israelites associated it with God's monumental act of saving them from Egypt after four hundred years of slavery. In Greek, Joshua translates, "Jesus." When a son was named Joshua, it was probably done with honor to the Lord and in the hope that the boy might develop Christlike qualities. Of course, Jesus was named by his legal father, Joseph, upon divine direction (Matthew 1:18-21). He was called Jesus of Nazareth by His contemporaries to distinguish Him from the number of others named Jesus in those days.

By Commitment to Something Worthwhile

During his lifetime, Joshua entered into certain relationships which aided him in committing his life to the worthwhile. First, Joshua had a meaningful, indelible relationship with the Lord. Joshua 5:13-15 details the incident near Jericho which affected his early manhood and lasted throughout his life.

This is the principle to be gained from the snapshot of that great day in Joshua's life: to understand what really counts among the many options before us, we need to know the Lord. We must know Him impressively, at the deepest level of our being. Through our deepening relationship with God, we are able to commit ourselves to the worthwhile. Through this holy association we are given the wisdom of the Lord.

Joshua also had made a commitment to Moses. As a younger man, he had been chosen to be Moses' personal servant (Exodus 24:12,13). As he helped the great emancipator in many tasks which needed doing, Joshua learned values from Moses. What Moses saw as important Joshua learned to consider important.

It matters whose disciple we become. Be careful whom you follow. We are what and whom we admire, love, honor and follow. We must thoughtfully, prayerfully determine our life's commitments. Joshua was a wise leader in later life because he had been a wise follower in earlier life.

Joshua's relationship with his contemporary, Caleb, also was instrumental in his commitment to the worthwhile (Numbers 14:6-10,38). He and

Caleb became friends and fellow spies. Caleb was a good influence on Joshua because he trusted God's Word and promises and desired to attempt great things in His name. The two young men were spiritually compatible, thereby strengthening each other's faith and high resolve. Isn't it sobering to realize that usually we adopt the values of those we make our closest friends? We have good intentions of lifting them to our principles, but often we compromise to theirs. If this happens, our ability to be dedicated to what is worthwhile diminishes. In friendship, as in leadership, we must make careful choices. Our friends have great ability to impact our lives.

Through Joshua's early life commitments he was enabled to arrive at the supreme commitment. This is the way he put it: "As for me and my house, we will serve the Lord." That was the bottom line for successful living as far as our Hebrew hero is concerned.

Joshua 24:14,15 suggests that the commitment to serve the Lord requires turning away from other things we may have set up as gods in our lives. We have to expel them with harshness and finality. Christ put the issue clearly: "No man can serve two masters." The Lord and the Lord alone must be God. Then, according to Joshua's statement the Lord is to be feared—that is, seriously and reverently worshiped. A constant, close relationship with Him is to be cultivated. Worship, so important to this high commitment, includes heartfelt praise to God, expressed thanksgiving for who He is and what He does, and learning more of His will and word.

At the core of, "as for me and my house, we will serve the Lord," is an active involvement in what God is doing in our time. This is a commitment to work for Him, a commitment to using the abilities He has given us. Since it is His desire that the whole world hear the good news of His love in Jesus Christ, ours is a commitment to the spreading of that gospel. He is bringing into being His eternal family. We who are committed to serving the Lord will do what we can to aid in this project. All service springs from an available, willing servant who doesn't seek personal acclaim. He pursues the great objective of making Christ known, first where he lives, branching out as God leads.

The process of commitment begins with an act of the will, a choice consciously and deliberately made. A decision is called for. Every enticement to delay must be set aside. We must exercise the will and step forward. We must move off dead center, using our ability to choose in its noblest exercise, to make a commitment to that which is worthwhile.

Making a commitment is also an act of leadership. What we do influences others. Seeing someone courageous and wise enough to take such a step encourages others to do the same. It may be exactly what one needs to move him into a life of highest joy. Joshua mentions "me and my house" in this respect. As parents, one of our most significant places of leadership is with our children. They don't know what goals in life to set for themselves until we tell them by word and example. As a child watches Father and Mother, he should hear them saying, "This is what's worthwhile in life. Follow me!"

In the marriage relationship many wives are looking for this leadership in their husbands. The good provider supplies spiritual direction and encouragement to living on the highest plane, as well as the material things life requires. Aimless, deteriorating marriages might be put back on a sure path if the man of the home would show commitment to what is worthwhile. Still, there are instances when a wife must pioneer the way. We may never know how far-reaching the influence of a mother can be when she is immovably dedicated to the worthwhile and is teaching her children accordingly.

A final point regarding commitment deserves to be made. Joshua's commitment was publicly known. By making one's decision known, one's determination is reinforced. It adds strength to resolve. It lends endurance to the commitment.

Chapter 7

By Discovering
Who Jesus Is

Enjoy Living . . .
   By Discovering Who Jesus Is

Human beings were designed for a meaningful relationship with God. Therefore, our life's most serious quest should be to discover who He is and what He does for us. Jesus makes this kind of knowledge possible. But such a small percentage of men and women experience this privilege! Is it any wonder so many fail to grasp true enjoyment?

Perhaps we can be helped along to discovering Jesus if we consider how Peter accomplished it. Peter has been admired and respected by millions for about two thousand years. Perhaps we take to him so quickly because he is so like us. Even through severe ups and downs, he remained an admirable character. He was not perfect but he usually gave his best. He was indeed mercurial but he was also vigorous and aggressive. He worked hard and progressed in his vocation, as well as in the business of living in general.

Matthew 16:13-17 gives us the account of the day Peter seriously discovered Jesus and clearly articulated his discovery. The fellow had had many great days in his life but this day was the greatest. And his discovery permeated all of his subsequent life. It isn't any wonder he is mentioned first in every list of the apostles in Scripture.

Peter made his discovery of Jesus in Caesarea Philippi, northeast of Galilee, a beautiful part of the territory known well by the big fisherman. Philip, the governor of that part of the Middle East, wanted to make sure he was on the good side of the Roman emperor, Caesar Augustus, so he built a city and named it after the monarch.

Jesus had taken His apostles to Caesarea Philippi for a time of quiet, serenity and privacy. With snow-capped Mount Hermon as a backdrop, this lovely retreat area was a good place in which to do some serious teaching. The area also provided Him an opportunity to rest up for the big ordeal immediately ahead of Him. In not too many days Jesus would stand trial before both the Jewish tribunal and Rome's Pilate. Then the authorities would nail Him to a cross.

However, we don't need a special setting to discover who Jesus is. All that is necessary is a genuine desire to know Him. He meets honest people in many places on life's path. Some paths are lovely and others are not so attractive. A heart and mind can reach out to Jesus any time. Waiting for what we perceive to be the right moment could be foolish. Who knows what other things might intrude to prevent our discovery? Where you are right now is the appropriate point of beginning.

Peter discovered that Jesus wants to be known person-to-person. In fact, He takes the initiative. Impressively, the Heavenly Father joins in the process of knowing Jesus. This is indicated in Christ's informative word to Peter, "And Jesus answered and said unto him, Blessed art thou, Simon Bar-jona: for flesh and blood hath not revealed it unto thee, but my Father which is in heaven" (Matthew 16:17).

It is such good news that the greatest Person you'll ever encounter wants you to know Him. Jesus came into the world to reveal eternal things, not hide them. And discovering Him is at the center of that revelation. Read Matthew, Mark, Luke and John prayerfully, telling Jesus you want to know Him. You'll be surprised at what happens because you and He are on the same wavelength. And remember, it doesn't matter who you are. He wants to be discovered by all of us.

In addition to wanting us to know Him, Jesus wants our knowledge of Him to be firsthand. Like in Matthew's story (16:13-17), what we get from someone else could be wrong. Jesus wasn't John the Baptist, Elijah, Jeremiah or any other prophet. However, if the apostles had accepted the conclusions of other people, that's what they would have believed. Don't settle for anything less than your own personal research on the subject of Jesus Christ. You have every right—in fact, every responsibility—to do this. Even though it will take time and serious study, nothing was ever more important than discovering who Jesus is for yourself.

One of the most significant things Peter learned about Jesus was that He was the Christ. In Jewish terms, the word "Christ" is more a description of Jesus than a name. For the Hebrew people, Jesus meant Messiah. The Old Testament has many thoughts about the Messiah. Certain of these are outstanding. For instance, the Christ is the chosen bearer of God's loving message to mankind. Jesus has made clear to us the Heavenly Father's message. This is partly why Jesus is called, "The Word" by the Christian Hebrew, John. He declares, "In the beginning was the Word, and the Word was with God, and the Word was God . . . And the Word was made flesh, and dwelt among us, (and we beheld his glory, the glory as of the only begotten of the Father,) full of grace and truth" (John 1:1,14).

As the Word, Jesus makes known God's reasoning through the Bible; He is the expression of God's divine thought process. Just as our words are vehicles by which we tell others what we are thinking, so Jesus is what God is thinking about the whole world in general, and you in particular. In brief, what God is thinking is this: you are worth all His love. God loves you just as you are, and will reach into your life and become a part of you and your experiences if you will let Him. The writer of the Book of Hebrews declares Christ is God's message bearer: "God, who at sundry times and in divers manners spake in time past unto the fathers by the prophets, hath in these last days spoken unto us by his Son" (Hebrews 1:1,2a).

Peter also learned that the Messiah became the Servant of Jehovah, a Servant who would suffer and die for the sins of the world. Isaiah 52:13—53:12 should be read seriously and repeatedly at this point. The information contained therein is indispensable in knowing Jesus. Then, read the latter parts of the four Gospels to see just how this prophecy worked out in history. We've discovered a really great Person and Friend when we can say, "He did this for me!" Our sins, wrongs, iniquities, griefs and sorrowful experiences He has made His own. He has effectively taken care of what we can't handle. One is not alone in life when he discovers Jesus.

The term "Christ" includes a further, exciting quality: Jesus is God's anointed King whose visible and beneficent rulership will cover the whole world some day. We live in days that are terribly confused in so many ways. It seems we've gone past the point of no return. Human ingenuity cannot produce a sufficient remedy. But don't give up! Jesus is heaven's Monarch who will return to the earth and put things back on track. In fact, He will restore all God's creation to that which He originally planned. God wants us to be so sure of this fact that He has spoken on this subject as much if not more than on any other subject in the Bible. Jesus is everlasting, victorious royalty!

When we put everything together, nothing is greater than what Peter says to Jesus, "You are the Son of the living God." This is ascription of deity. "Son" is not used in an inferior sense; rather, to indicate Jesus possesses all the qualities of the Lord God Almighty. As a staunch, orthodox, monotheistic Hebrew, it took much study for Peter to come to this decision. You can be confident he was sure before he said such a thing. Peter had lived with Jesus in all situations. He had talked with Him personally hours on end. He had seen the tears Jesus shed over the needs of people. Before his eyes, he saw miracles repeatedly performed by Jesus. Peter had seen Jesus worn out due to the pressures of life. Once Jesus was so tired He slept through a rough storm on the Sea of Galilee. When Peter had taken all his experiences with Jesus into account and evaluated what He was, there was only one conclusion—Jesus is divine.

This discovery colored all of Peter's later life. He died as a martyr because he would not give up what he knew to be true. When we learn Jesus is God, it will change our lives too. The future takes on new hope. Service in His name becomes very significant for we are ministering to none less than the Lord. We are not playing games; we are doing something meaningful. His friendship and companionship assure us we can face whatever living may bring. Worshiping

Him makes sense; it is worthwhile since He is God.

It is indispensable to joyful living that we personally and properly answer Jesus' inquiry, "But what about you? Who do you say I am?" As we go through life we will have many crisis hours. Absolutely no one is exempt. In these times, particularly, we must have a firm, unshakable grip on Christ's person. It will produce in us what Paul delighted in when He declared, "For the which cause I also suffer these things: nevertheless I am not ashamed: for I know whom I have believed, and am persuaded that he is able to keep that which I have committed unto him against that day" (II Timothy 1:12).

For a cup of life that runs over, discover who Jesus is! The sooner the better! You can't afford to ignore Him.

Chapter 8

By Entering A
Rewarding Partnership

Enjoy Living . . .
By Entering a Rewarding Partnership

The 1980s and 90s may prove to be the decades of the space shuttle. After more than ten years of hard work and billions of dollars, the shuttle has arrived to stay. *Columbia* astronaut Robert L. Crippen exclaimed, "This is the world's greatest flying machine." The space shuttle is a marvel of technological achievement. In its entirety, it is eighteen stories high and weighs 4.5 million pounds. It reaches speeds of 17,000 miles per hour, but most awesome of all are the shuttle's computer components with the magnificent four primary computers, a backup and a spare. The four primary computers are programmed to perform identically. Each of them could operate the ship alone, but each of the four provides a check on the others. Should the four disagree on a course of action, the backup computer will step in and make the decision. These machines talk to each other constantly, making as many as 440 checks every second.

Though this technological sophistication and practical potential arouses our admiration and excitement, there is one ingredient without which it could not happen—partnership. Not hundreds of people going their own way and doing their own thing. But scores of gifted people with varied skills working together. There must be partnership on the teams of astronauts who are blasted into orbit. Partnership between the computers aboard. Partnership between the space people and the computers. Partnership between computers and those who program them. Partnership between the personnel orbiting the earth and personnel at Mission Control in Houston. Even partnership between everyone in the space program and us taxpayers who sponsor the program. It won't work without interdependence.

This is true of life in general. None of us can go it alone, regardless how strong our independent spirit. For life to bring us joy, we must have the invigoration that partnership brings. When God created man He made him a social creature. Thus, meaningful interaction with other people is indispensable to his fulfillment. Likewise, the Trinity does not live in isolation, but in constant companionship; and from this relationship the salvation of souls has become a reality. So it isn't surprising that human beings made in the divine likeness should thrive on partnership.

For maximum benefit, however, that companionship must be of the right sort. Our purpose now is to see what this proper partnership is.

Going back to the beginning of the Bible record, we find our source of specific information in Genesis 1:26,27. When God brought male and female into existence He entered them upon a life of enjoyment through partnership. God called both sexes "man." Both were made in the image of God. Both were equally given the privilege of living life to the fullest. Therefore, both must seek partnership if their cup is to run over. Scripture suggests this rewarding partnership is a simultaneous activity in at least three areas of human relationships.

The first harmonious relationship necessary is living in partnership with our physical environment. The most constant association Adam and Eve had each day was with their physical surroundings. The same is true for us. God's act of creation was based upon perfect wisdom. There is unity between all God has made. Both humanity and earth require the sensitive interaction of the other for their highest potential. Selfishness cannot intrude. True partnership is necessary. The physical environment is provided to sustain human beings. They, in turn, are to exercise careful, concerned, continuing mastership of their surroundings. The nature of the environment is to be harnessed by man but not destroyed in the process (Genesis 1:26-30).

In this time of conflict between environmentalists and industrialists, there must be an understanding by both of the partnership God has built into humanity and into man's surroundings. It is frightening to live in a highly technological society which forgets the two-way street of partnership. The result in both directions is extremism: one extreme which produces acid rain and hardly breathable air; and an equal extreme that seeks to preserve the snail darter at the expense of a man's making a living.

Balance must be sought between the human family and its home. The joy of the exploiter is short-lived. Yet, the sternness of those thoughtless of human necessity is outside God's intention for creation.

Both man and his environment have been pained by sin; they need each other for recovery. And one of these days both are going to be restored to that which God planned for them (Romans 8:21-23). That day is to be ushered in when Jesus reigns upon the earth. What a day that will be! Bursting with beauty, glory and life! And it may not be in the too-distant future. The human race and its environment cannot continue in their opposition to each other indefinitely.

The second partnership which is so crucial to our enjoyment of life is our communion with God. This partnership is shared with the Heavenly Father as a Person (friendship) and with Him in the functioning of His creation (business). See Genesis 2:4-6,15,19-20. Partners in friendship; partners in business— that covers a big chunk of life. And you can count on it to bring life a joyful fullness.

It is rather hard to grasp that a human being and God Almighty can be partners simply in sharing time together, isn't it? Partners, even in leisure time. The Lord and you sitting around a warm fire and talking. Or walking together in the country. Or having a conversation as you drive the freeways. This is how God originally wanted it to be. He never wanted it to end. The human sin factor turned everything around, restricted the partnership.

I can't imagine having a partnership in friendship with our President, to say nothing of a partnership with God! But this is what our Heavenly Father would like to establish with us. And it's really what we want deep in our hearts. None of us can escape that longing for the ultimate partnership in friendship.

It's wonderful that the Lord didn't leave us alone after sin had broken the bond. He made the second effort to revive what humanity had lost. First, He gave His Son to take our sin away, thereby eliminating our guilt and estrangement. With that done, a partnership in personal friendship can be formed. When a person comes to Christ as a sinner and welcomes Him into his life, he has done his part in advancing toward the partnership. Timothy tells the good news of this partnership-producing procedure by saying, "[God our Saviour] . . . will have all men to be saved, and to come unto the knowledge of the truth. For there is one God, and one mediator between God and men, the man Christ Jesus: who gave himself a ransom for all" (I Timothy 2:4-6a). Jesus Himself spoke of this aspect of His mission declaring, "I am the way, the truth, and the life: no man cometh unto the Father, but by me" (John 14:6).

Our partnership in friendship is enriched as we learn more of God's person through His Word. In a way the Bible is a holy autobiography. As we read it we are able to enter into new and different phases of the partnership until we find He can join us in every area of our Christian lives. Knowing Him better and having a clearer idea of how He operates deepens our involvement in this superb friendship. Of course, the Holy Spirit plays an important role in this because He is our accurate teacher. The Lord is the person He makes real and exalts. The Bible is His text. So we further our partnership by the Holy Spirit's dominance in our lives.

When, with all eagerness and sincerity we set out to build a partnership in friendship with God, when we follow the path to it which He has marked out, we can be assured we will achieve the coveted goal of friendship.

A final partnership opportunity is suggested in the Genesis story—that of living in partnership with Eve, the mate God gave Adam (Genesis 2:18-25). Of all human associations, that of husband and wife is most important. Therefore, it is to be carefully and conscientiously built and maintained. Because marriage is the closest earth relationship approximating union with God, it has been dealt severely devastating blows by Satan. Homes around the world are reeling under the barrage.

By Entering A Rewarding Partnership

Basic to creating a strong partnership is evaluating the persons in it as God evaluates them. Man and woman have a basic alikeness and stand on the level ground of equality. In fact, the word "woman" may mean "female man." The two words stress fundamental alikeness. "So God created man in his own image, in the image of God created he him; male and female created he them" (Genesis 1:27). A husband and wife have distinctive roles in their marriage but as to their persons they are equal and, therefore, partners.

What is more, they unavoidably need each other. There is no such thing as detachment in a healthy marriage. The Lord described Eve whom He made from Adam's rib as a helper suitable for him (Genesis 2:18). A wife is one who so complements her husband, is so much his counterpart that, in partnership, they develop a unity in their relationship.

Scripture speaks of a spirit of total commitment which must be present for a marriage to survive. "Cleaving" speaks of an unbreakable union. So complete is the interpenetration of the committed persons in marriage that they are called "one flesh." This does not refer to their physical beings only. They are one body, soul, emotion and spirit. Given this tremendous joining of two people, nothing less than true partnership can complement their marriage.

Today, when varied vocational opportunities are available to both husband and wife, there is a danger of husband and wife going their own separate ways. We must walk together as partners, or there is no joy in marriage.

Chapter 9

By Keeping Your Personal Integrity

Enjoy Living . . .
By Keeping Your Personal Integrity

There are many ways to measure wealth. A little boy with a couple of hundred toy soldiers may feel very wealthy. But his dad would have an entirely different evaluation. So if you were asked how rich you consider yourself to be, your answer may or may not be impressive to another. It depends on our standard of values.

How truly well-to-do are you? In most cultures materialism is a gauge toward determining wealth. The Navajo living in Northern Arizona or New Mexico is considered well off if he has a good-sized flock of sheep. His tribe counts up its wealth in terms of coal reserves or uranium mines.

The sophisticated suburbanite refers to his investment folder when calculating his worth. With housing so expensive across America, possession of a home and land may declare one's wealth.

It is often said that the person who has his health is rich. Being physically well is basic to whatever life may require of us. Being strong in body is a real treasure.

Since most people are achievement-conscious, the vocationally successful person is considered wealthy. There is something admirable about an individual who so applies himself to his calling that he rises to the top. That carpenter, doctor, accountant or secretary who has gained personal satisfaction by a job well done is possessed of an inner wealth hard to describe.

Good interpersonal relationships can make one rich. Looking at the fine children of many parents, one has to declare those mothers and fathers wealthy. And what a treasure it is to have true friends in whom you can confide and with whom you can share life's highest experiences. Being surrounded by people who care is a great treasure. There are men and women who are wealthy because of their talents. Divine Providence has provided a genetic structure which has bestowed upon them enviable talents and abilities.

Each of these categories has true worth. None is to be thought of lightly for each brings special value. But there is something which is of greater value than all other successes. It can be owned by human beings of any culture, any age, any nationality, any social position. He who has personal integrity is really wealthy. Integrity produces a life of wonderful joy and fulfillment. It brings a clear conscience, a sense of rightness about ourselves which is worth more than monetary wealth. With integrity one can face his world and calmly look it straight in the eye.

Integrity is that quality in an individual which makes him or her trustworthy and reliable. It is a quality which makes others feel confident and secure. His word is good; his life reflects the best standards of conduct. There are no subtleties in him—no footnotes in small print that will bring disappointment or disillusionment.

It is essential we be alert to those areas in which our integrity is severely threatened. One of the most obvious threats is to our moral integrity, particularly where sex is concerned.

Bend every effort to keep your sexual integrity. We must get this message across to junior high, high school and college people whose moral health will determine the character of our future. Once one loses his sexual integrity, it is rarely ever regained. Towering over all peer pressures and social entice- ments to a lowering of one's moral life, God stands to help those who turn to Him. When they waver, He is strong. God and you can keep your integrity!

Because there has so often been an absence of professional integrity in the spheres of business and politics, thousands of people have become skeptics. Little integrity is seen in commodity advertising. Politicians as a group are distrusted. The remedy for this situation is a return on every level to integrity.

Such a return can be accomplished when business and social leadership are open to God and His way. To bring this about, a serious acceptance of the Bible and action on its statements of proper values and principles are necessary.

An excellent example of personal integrity is found in Joseph, son of Jacob. Genesis 37—50 comprise the relevant data on him. Joseph was a truly great person. It is puzzling that he isn't mentioned in the New Testament at all. He possessed such enviable qualities that at thirty years of age he was appointed by the King of Egypt to be second in command over all that highly civilized country. His responsibilities were great and he carried them out expertly. Yet he was approachable by the citizens of Egypt.

Joseph had the highest respect for his father and showed it. Though his brothers had grossly mistreated him he forgave them with a loving, generous spirit. The young governor returned good for evil. He had a magnificent philosophy of life, believing in God's kind providence even in very adverse situations. Almost anyone would have been happy and proud to have Joseph as a son, or husband, or father, or brother.

Though he was a man of talent, character and ability, Joseph was not exempt from circumstances which sorely tested his integrity (Genesis 39:1-20). An integrity crisis may well arise in the course of our daily routine. Usually, the problem isn't suddenly upon us, full-blown. It builds bit by bit. We must be sensitive to what's going on around us daily. I don't mean we are to be suspicious of everybody and everything, nor withdraw from relationships, but we must be alert to things which might be influencing our thoughts and decisions. We recognize elements which might chip away at our integrity. Living in companionship with the Lord will give wise insights into what subtleties may be influencing us, and He will supply strength to overcome them.

Joseph's experience with his boss's wife is similar to crises we may face in that the sniping at our integrity is persistent. Temptation doesn't stop after one try. It picks and nibbles at us day in and day out. And it pleads, "Just this time." Satan knows that once our integrity has been violated it will be easier next time. Often this happens in a way we're hardly conscious of. Take, as a case in point, the words of some contemporary songs which are constantly poured into the heads of our youth. Words about sex, violence, drugs. Well-meaning young people may say, "The words don't affect me. I like the beat." But those words *do* affect them subconsciously. That which often results is smashed integrity. Here again, vital and practical contact with God is priceless. His Word and our faith in Him act as a buffer. Faith can be the bulletproof glass protecting our integrity.

Don't miss the truth that this battle is most often waged where you're most vulnerable. Joseph was a young, well-built, handsome, virile man. He was vulnerable in the area of strong sex drive. And that is the point where his integrity came under fire. The sex drive isn't wrong; it's how one handles the drive that matters. But this is just one area. Some people are vulnerable where money is concerned. Or prestige and acceptance. Or pride. Too often we'll do anything to be satisfied in our vulnerable spot. We must be honest with ourselves and know where we will be most susceptible to a compromise of integrity.

Joseph reacted in his time of testing with a wisdom all of us can copy. If we adopt the philosophy of acting responsibly because others are trusting us, it will run counter to the popular idea that all that matters is what satisfies us. Such a self-serving ideology will destroy our integrity every time. However, feeling there is a responsible way to act because somebody is putting faith in us will help keep our integrity clear. Whether we like it or not, others are being affected by the way we live. Once our integrity is diminished and trust is broken, it may be a long time before they can be restored.

To maintain and strengthen integrity, one must act in keeping with God's standards. In a real way, sacrificing our integrity is a sin against Him in that it is a violation of the values He has set for the human family. But a desire to please God gives an individual strength he can get from no other source. He seems to draw on hidden inner resources which enable the Lord's power to bear also.

Need it be said that one of the most important instruments in maintaining personal integrity is the determined refusal to compromise? At times we must say a resounding, "No!" to temptation. It's not always bad to be negative. Often this requires the resolve of Jesus who after forty days and nights of fasting fought off the fiercest of Satan's attempts to get Him to swerve from right. Christ will help you in your battle if you will enlist His aid.

Once you have refused to give in, you will do well to flee from the danger if possible. It is most unwise to tease the imps committed to our defeat. Being negative must be followed by being positive. Move away from the potential danger as quickly as possible. Run for your life! Associate with people, attitudes and life-styles which will be supportive of your determination. Any life that retains integrity of person is well worth living. It brings a very special sort of enjoyment and effectiveness into who you are and what you do.

Chapter 10

By Getting
Outside Yourself

Enjoy Living . . .
By Getting Outside Yourself

There is a unique and innovative place near Orlando, Florida called Circus World. Here not only will you see a fine circus, but you are given the chance to try out your ability in some of the acts. With a welcome safety net beneath, you may see how you do on the flying trapeze. Jugglers will teach your children how to juggle. Or maybe they'd rather be painted up like clowns and have their picture taken. Should you volunteer, the people of Circus World will put a strap around your waist, snap the strap to a strong cable and let you try your hand at walking the tightrope. Most everybody teeters and falls. Harmless circus fun. Perhaps this area of the circus is so much fun because, given the chance, we all like to act out some of our childhood fantasies.

Getting outside oneself at Circus World is symbolic of what we all must go through in the process of living. For a full life every one of us must walk the tightrope between a proper occupation with ourselves and getting outside ourselves. We cannot fully enjoy life as long as we are the center of our own every thought, word, decision and action.

In order to determine whether or not you are preoccupied with self, consider these questions. When you meet people for the first time do you consciously or unconsciously steer the conversation so that it revolves around you—your job, your house, children, family history? Or do you encourage your new acquaintance to share his life—where he is from, what he has done, his hopes, number of children? Honestly answering these questions can be quite revealing. In fact, it may tell you whether or not yours is presently a rich, full and enjoyable life.

As a biblical pacesetter in getting outside oneself, let's look at Moses. What a leader he was! He directed about three million Hebrew slaves out of bondage to Egypt, the most powerful, advanced civilization of the time. Then he guided this huge company through the hot sands of the Sinai Desert until, decades later, they came to the land of their destiny. Can you imagine the logistics of an undertaking that size? How would one provide food and water for them—to say nothing of meeting all their other needs! Think of the persistence it took when things got rough. Think of the organization it required. It was like moving one of the world's largest cities! History has never seen a thing like this before or since Moses. And without him it would have collapsed into the greatest failure ever witnessed by man.

However, this successful exodus could not have been carried out unless Moses had been able to get outside himself. Some personality traits could have made him just the opposite of what he had to be as a successful leader. For instance, Moses was basically a meek character. By nature he was quite mild. This sort of person is retiring. He steps back and lets someone else do the job because he is shy. He is willing to live in his own little world. This reticence seemed to flow deeply in Moses' nature (Numbers 12:1-3). Since the Bible does not exaggerate, it is worth noting that Moses is described as "very meek, above all the men which are upon the face of the earth."

But he did not allow his lack of aggressiveness to keep him from moving into God's will, to keep him from taking his place in God's program. We cannot afford to have this happen in our lives either. One wonders how many times in the course of his life Moses had to take himself in hand to get outside himself. You may need to be this determined and disciplined too. Getting outside yourself may not be easy; it may be very contrary to your makeup. But if reticence and withdrawal are keeping you from your part in God's plan, you must do it. Don't excuse yourself into ineffectiveness.

Besides being passive, Moses was not a very

good communicator. He proved this by the way he evidently bungled an attempt to show the Israelis he was really on their side (Exodus 2:11-14). In fact, the episode became the cause of his self-exile from Egypt. In addition to being a poor communicator, Moses was not a good speaker. He may have had a speech impediment, but speaking was very necessary to the job God had asked him to do (Exodus 4:10-12). Handicaps like this must not keep you from stepping forward to accept God's call, just as they did not stop Moses. As God told Moses, He's the One who will give what is necessary to meet the requirements of His will. You must not turn around and become withdrawn, for this may be when your most exciting relationship with God occurs.

Moses had a lot of advantages and possessions. These comforts could have hindered him in the Lord's work. He was very well educated and could enrich his intellectual attainments in Egypt's libraries and at the feet of her best educators. Culturally, he had available the finest Egyptian civilization could offer. In addition he had been trained in the practical aspects of living. Too, he was the grandson of the King of Egypt.

Though there are some exceptions, we are a people with advantages similar to those of Moses. Perhaps not in the same quantity, but we have culture and education available to us, too. We must not so feed upon these assets that we shut the door on self-disclosure. We should thank God for what we have, but also remember that He intends that these things should motivate us to reach out. We must not permit our blessings to entomb us within ourselves. Rather, they should be wings carrying us into the world of people. One never really has a fully joyful life without sharing his personhood with others.

Having noted some hindrances to getting outside oneself, suppose we touch on some positive factors. Even with his hindrances, Moses moved away from self-preoccupation. How did he do it? How can we do it? Privately, Moses committed himself to God. Nothing spiritually spectacular nor public happened. The transaction was deep—between God and Moses on personal, sacred territory. But it permanently sent him outside himself with the ability to make a difference in his society and biblical history.

Hebrews 11:24-27 describes some of Moses' inner convictions. More insight is given in these verses about the man and his exploits than are given in the Old Testament. Determination was one of Moses' most basic positive qualities. When the moment of truth came, Moses chose to move outside himself and on to the needs of Israel. The path to rich living begins at this point. We want to do something which will lead us outside ourselves. A full life will not come against a person's will. Neither will the apathetic individual achieve it. How was Moses able to get outside the confines of self and do a work for God? He trusted that God's way was best. It must have looked like folly to those who knew the man. Why would he refuse all that being a part of

Pharaoh's immediate family meant? Moses must have been out of his mind, some thought. Though looking out for "number one" seems to be most immediately satisfying, long-term joy comes when an individual will believe God and get outside himself. It's a step of faith that is built upon the solid direction of the Lord.

The verses in Hebrews show that Moses accomplished his objective by becoming a part of the people of God, no matter what the cost. This interaction will lift any person out of himself and into human needs. The philosophy of Christianity is that believers in Christ are to touch others and help them to God. This is the way Jesus saw His mission; therefore, He died on a cross for the world. Anyone in whom this Saviour lives as Lord will have the same approach to life. He cannot live only for himself. To live in the fullest joy and sense of achievement, we must let Christ in.

Too, Moses caught the excitement of investing his life in an eternal, divine purpose. The Heavenly Father is about the business of bringing people into the family of the redeemed. When our values are properly in line, we will want to invest our lives in partnership with God in this enterprise. We're not promised an easy task. The "reproach of Christ" will always be a part of our efforts. But when we join God in what He's doing, we'll be lifted out of ourselves. In our vocation, we need to view it as a way to unite with God in helping people become a part of His family through the Lord Jesus Christ.

Moses understood that God rewards those who are associated with Him in His objective. When Moses got hold of that thought, he was never again the same man. We're not being unspiritual when we anticipate the rewards the Lord has promised His own for their fidelity to Him and His cause. It's valid to expect a payday in heaven. Of course, the Bible says we will gladly declare that whatever we receive has been by the Lord's grace and power. Crowns will be cast at His feet. All glory will be attributed to Him. But that doesn't do away with the truth that God wants to give us recompense. And He's going to do it!

There is a special place in the everlasting city of God for dedicated, working Christians (Hebrews 11:8-10; 12:22; 13:14; Revelation 21:1-3). When you get a glimpse of the potential ahead of you, you'll want to get out of yourself and to the work God has for you. Nowhere can you hope for a higher return on the investment of your life. For whom are you really working? Have you calculated who pays the best?

The Hebrews passage emphasizes that Moses kept his attention and affection focused on God. You must not lose sight of the wonder of His person. When your eyes are fixed on this, the sight will move you outside yourself and you will continue on the right path. Perhaps people along the way will be of little encouragement to you. Indeed, they may be downright discouraging. No doubt you'll face some days of rough going when you wonder if it wouldn't be better to crawl back into your shell. But if you get a picture of the Lord's worthiness, you'll be able to stay with the task by following His example. So, cultivate your devotional life. Keep God clearly in your vision. It's the secret to success in every other part of living.

Two Old Testament stories about Moses combine to teach us a lesson: be a person who seriously and persistently prays for others. Even when they are unworthy of your concern (Exodus 32:9-14,30-35; Numbers 14:11-21; Deuteronomy 9:23-29). This kind of involvement is both a command of Christ (Luke 6:28) and a following of His example (Luke 23:34). One who takes this advice seriously soon gets outside himself. He cannot be prayerfully wrapped up in the pain of others and wrapped up in himself at the same time. This is Christian love flowing out to people and rising heavenward to God.

No one contradicts the fact that we make contact with some pretty sorry characters daily. However, instead of brooding over these distasteful relationships until they fill you with self-pity, talk to God about and for them. Perhaps one of your family or closest friends has hurt you the most. No matter! You must pray! You will be surprised how much better you will feel, and your prayer allows God to begin working in them. All circumstances can be helped by prayer. Then let God take over the job! Plead for His glory in these hard experiences. Ask that His Word and witness be honored in your world and among your contemporaries. This is exactly what Moses did and he found it successful. You too will see some fine things come to pass!

Chapter 11

By Being Yourself

Enjoy Living . . .
By Being Yourself

The scene was London. The date: July 29, 1981. Beautiful St. Paul's Cathedral hosted the majestic happening. Celebrities the world over were there. The rest of us were too, thanks to television and satellite communication. The royal wedding was a happy day for millions, a welcome time of relaxation in a tense world.

Britain was delighted with the choice their Prince Charles had made. Lovely Diana had charmed staid England. Her wedding to Prince Charles brought back memories of an empire that hadn't existed for thirty years. The romance, the pomp, the pageantry of it! Sometimes we need a refreshing bath in memories. To the English, the royal wedding was a matter of spirit, not logic.

One wonders how many women would like to be like "Shy Di." Perhaps not only be like her, but actually be her. It isn't so much that they want what she has—her eighteen carat sapphire ring set in a fourteen diamond garland, or a husband whose annual income, exempt from income tax, is $1.25 million. They just want to be what she *is*. Her hairstyle has been widely copied almost since the announcement of her engagement. Her clothes are being imitated, both in England and countries thousands of miles away. The exclamation, "Oh, you look like Princess Diana" is coveted.

Many people want to be someone other than who they are. As long as that desire dominates a person's thinking and hopes, there can be no true, full joy in living. Each of us must accept himself or herself in order to begin to enjoy living from a sound, healthy base. We also must be ourselves for God. Out of this combination of attitudes, a pleasing, purposeful life develops.

Little children often identify with their parents. They often play "house," playing "mother" or "dad." They clomp around in high-heeled shoes or try to talk in a deeper, man's voice. This role identification is necessary to growing up; an early step in easing oneself into a mature world. Psychologists sometimes encourage role playing as part of therapy. And the Bible urges the children of God to become so much a part of the lives of those who struggle that we enter the condition with them. Hebrews 13:3 says, "Remember them that are in bonds, as bound with them; and them which suffer adversity, as being yourselves also in the body." But this encouragement to living an involved life is not an invitation to try to become another person.

The principle of being yourself for God doesn't deny the fact that you may need to make changes in your life where they are indicated. Every individual must constantly desire to be a better person. But, when by faith one opens his life to Jesus Christ, he becomes someone new in the finest sense of the word. Paul puts it this way: "Therefore if any man be in Christ, he is a new creature: old things are passed away; behold, all things are become new" (II Corinthians 5:17). In the same spirit he wrote to Titus: "But after that the kindness and love of God our Saviour toward man appeared, not by works of righteousness which we have done, but according to his mercy he saved us, by the washing of regeneration, and renewing of the Holy Ghost; which he shed on us abundantly through Jesus Christ our Saviour; that being justified by his grace, we should be made heirs according to the hope of eternal life" (Titus 3:4-7). Consider especially the words, "renewing of the Holy Ghost." God makes such a change in our persons when we trust His Son, but we are still the same individuals. He wants it that way.

Turn your thinking from the spiritual to the physical. Many of us need to make physical changes. We need to do something about matters of the body over which we have control. For instance, consider the lady who was so overweight that when she applied for a job her first consideration was whether or not she could squeeze through the door of the ladies' room! She needed to make some physical alterations. But even if she lost 150 pounds, she would still be the same person.

This principle carries over to the spiritual realm also. A Christian is, or should be, always in the process of development and maturity. God's intention for each one of His children is that they become ever more like Christ. All the experiences He permits in life have that positive purpose in mind. Much of the activity of the Holy Spirit in a Christian moves toward that goal. A thought-provoking verse in this regard is, "But we all, with open face beholding as in a glass the glory of the Lord, are changed into the same image from glory to glory, even as by the Spirit of the Lord" (II Corinthians 3:18).

One of these happy days Jesus is going to come back from heaven to take Christians there. Those who have died will have their bodies resurrected and living Christians will be snatched up into the clouds just as they are. Both groups will be changed right down to the final person. They'll be made like Christ. (Read Philippians 3:20,21; I Thessalonians 4:13-18; I Corinthians 15:51-53.) But even this transformation will not take away the Christian's identifiable individuality. You will still be yourself. The distinctive soul that entered the world at birth will go on that way with the Lord forever.

What God doesn't intend to change, we shouldn't

attempt to change either. To the contrary, we must try with His help to be the best person we can be. And we should try to accomplish this in a way that honors the Lord who thinks so much of us personally.

There is sound reasoning from Scripture for this attitude of just being yourself. David states a most amazing thing about each of us in Psalm 139:13-18. God knew you and what you would be from the moment you were conceived in your mother's body. In fact, He guided your development until your birth. It is not too much to say that there never has been, there isn't now, and there never will be anyone just like you—not even if you are an identical twin. God in His perfect love and wisdom let you become yourself for His own eternal, compassionate purposes. You are one of a kind with a mission to fulfill in your generation which no one else can accomplish. An important question is, Do you value yourself as the Lord does? Do you see yourself in the same spirit of mission in the world that He does?

At this point we should know and lay claim to a couple of treasured Christian doctrines: God's providence and God's grace. In His providence, God has brought you and circumstance into the world at a certain time to meet a specific need. You are who you are as a part of God's holy plan. As you join with God in His plan, He will continue His full providential care for you. If you doubt your uniqueness, His grace will give you strength to make something positive out of your self-imposed limitations. Remember God's providence! The Lord is up to something wonderful! Count on His gracious ability to overcome seemingly limiting factors. Your life is not out of control. Personally apply II Corinthians 12:7-10 to your situation, as Paul did.

In looking for a biblical character who might illustrate the point of being oneself, we read about a man who is mentioned in three of the four Gospels. Although unnamed, he was important to Christ at a crucial time in the Saviour's life; he had a real place in the plan of God for the salvation of the world (Matthew 26:17-19; Mark 14:12-16; Luke 22:7-13).

Though the man was special to Christ, his name was not recorded. He is called, "a man," "the owner," "him," and "he." But the apostles and Christ owe the gracious environment of the upper room to this person. What blessed things happened there—not the least of them being Jesus' institution of the Communion Supper. Some of Christ's most meaningful words were spoken there. The deepest emotions of the twelve men who would change the world were stirred in the room the unnamed man had provided.

To the world at large, most of us are no-names. Maybe we're mentioned in the local newspaper's birth notices and obituary. But national fame doesn't come to most of us. However, to God we are not of small importance. What matters to Him is that we function as ourselves; that we take our place in His plan. One of these days He'll let all heaven in on who we are. Having a well-known name is not what matters. The fact of the matter is, God does the majority of His work upon earth through no-names such as ourselves. Read Paul's evaluation of our basic worth in I Corinthians 1:26-29.

From Scripture, we assume that the man without a name and the owner of the house where Jesus met with the apostles were the same individual. There is no reason for rejecting that assumption. This being the case, it is possible the man was single because carrying water as he did was a woman's task in that day, often the task of a servant girl. If this man owned a house with a large upstairs guest room, perhaps was fairly well-to-do, it was unusual for him to be carrying the water. In addition, he had carried a pitcher or jar of water on his shoulder. Men usually carried leather bottles; women used the pottery jars. So we see a man who was being himself in his community.

Do you sometimes think you must change your personality somehow before you can be of service to the Lord? Not so! The best *you* is just what He wants—not some other person superimposed over you. Since our unnamed man may have been single, let's consider that for a moment. Like many other people, you may be a single person. You are not barred from spiritual effectiveness. God can work with you in a meaningful way. You have an important place in what God is doing in this generation. You are in no way inferior. Actually, Paul put a premium on singleness (I Corinthians 7:32,33). Whenever you feel that you are out of the mainstream of society, remember you're not out of the mainstream of God's plans.

The man with the house, as we'll call him, was tuned in to Jesus' thinking. He knew what the Saviour meant when He said, "My time is at hand" (Matthew 26:18). To be effective in being yourself it is essential that you live close to the Lord. Daily prayer and meditation are important prerequisites to knowing God's desires. You cannot afford to neglect your prayer life if you are to live the life of fullest joy. Dr. Richard C. Halverson, the fiftieth Chaplain of the United States Senate, has said, "I have a devotional life bcause I know that I need it . . . I have recaptured something that came to me early in my Christian experience—that Jesus Christ owns me because He created me, owns me because He purchased me with His sacrifice on the cross and has a right to possess me totally. I'd stop everything else before I'd stop my devotional life."

This man carrying the water jar down a Jerusalem street had the attitude of a servant and disciple. To him Jesus was the Master, the Teacher. In aspiring to be your finest, you must never let pride in what you are slip between you and Christ. Your calling can be used for His glory only when you exalt your Master and place all you are and have at His disposal. Showing His love through your life will glorify Him and enable you to bring your contemporaries toward faith in Him.

A person who is putting forth his best self for Christ will have all his talents and possessions at

God's disposal. The man's upper room was furnished. I can imagine that the carpets were clean, the cushions and couches were ready for the time of reclining and eating. Perhaps even a lamb for the Passover feast had been provided. Whatever the Lord needed, whenever He needed it, the man was ready to provide it. The man, in effect, said, as Abraham had said before him, "Behold, here I am" (Genesis 22:1); or as Ananias of Damascus had responded, "Behold, I am here, Lord" (Acts 9:10). God can use spirits like these. No wonder He did great things through them. If we be ourselves, and have our possessions in readiness, He will work through us also.

We observe that the man not only had the means to help Jesus; at Jesus' invitation he gladly completed the act of service. In his upper room Jesus instituted what we now call the Lord's Supper. This wonderful ordinance speaks of the supreme reason God's Son entered the world: to die for mankind's sins and rise triumphant from the grave. It is the story of the Saviour's sacrifice because of God's eternal love. What an effort in which to be involved!

This act took courage, though. In view of the prevailing antagonism of Jerusalem's leaders to Jesus, the man without a name was brave to take his place beside the Lord. Just how serious the threat was is indicated by the fact that the meal was held in secret and the address of the rendezvous wasn't given.

We do not know at what point our courage may

be tested because of our involvement with the Lord Jesus. We must persevere, knowing God has called us to this holy service and will stand with us as we stand for Him. You can count on it—the Lord will honor you for your commitment and courage. The unknown man's action will never be forgotten as long as the Bible endures. Today millions of people visit the spot in Jerusalem which is reported to be the location of the upper room.

We can have a rich life now and be an unforgotten—although perhaps unnamed—person forever. All because we are willing to be ourselves for God. Where could we ever find a better place to invest our unique selves?

Chapter 12

By Refusing to Run
From Difficulty

Enjoy Living . . .
By Refusing to Run from Difficulty

Whether in the first, faint rays of daylight or the final moments of twilight, you'll see them—a dedicated army of joggers. Their perspiring forms are a common sight in all seasons, during almost every kind of weather.

A change for the good has come across our land. We have become fitness-conscious. A Gallup poll taken not long ago revealed that about half of the total population is exercising daily. All forms of exercise personally benefit us. Exercise calms us mentally and emotionally. We get our minds off stressful problems for awhile.

Vigorous physical exercise aids us in venting our frustrations to some degree. At a certain point in strenuous exercise, euphoria is said to come over one, a sense of peace and well-being which he can get from no other source. Usually, however, emphasis is put on the physical dividends derived from consistent, vigorous exercise—increased capacity for endurance, improved energy, increase in weight loss and muscle tone.

In His Word, God concerns Himself with physical health also. Many of the laws He gave the Israelis had to do with maintenance of good health. But, aside from giving attention to physical exercise, at times Scripture likens life to running. "But they that wait upon the Lord shall renew their strength; they shall mount up with wings as eagles; they shall run, and not be weary; and they shall walk, and not faint" (Isaiah 40:31). "Know ye not that they which run in a race run all, but one receiveth the prize? So run, that ye may obtain" (I Corinthians 9:24). "Wherefore seeing we also are compassed about with so great a cloud of witnesses, let us lay aside every weight, and the sin which doth so easily beset us, and let us run with patience the race that is set before us" (Hebrews 12:1). "I returned, and saw under the sun, that the race is not to the swift" (Ecclesiastes 9:11a).

In our analogy, it is important to do more than run. We must be sure we are running in the right direction. More specifically, when difficulties meet us in life, we must be sure we do not retreat or we will not live a joy-filled life. When one faces these difficulties together with God, his cup overflows and he becomes stronger. Difficulties must be faced and successfully dealt with. Fortunately for us, the Bible gives insight as to how we may accomplish this.

Those who have read about him will agree with almost unanimous consent that Abraham was a most remarkable man. Uniquely, he is claimed as hero and father by the three major world religions: (1) Islam claims him through Ishmael; (2) Judaism through Isaac; and (3) Christianity sees him as the father of all who believe God's self-disclosure in Scripture and put faith in Jesus Christ, His Son.

This son of Terah from Ur of the Chaldees possessed personal greatness. He was a friend of God (Isaiah 41:8). He earned this enviable description by being faithful to God in almost every situation. He was so close to the Lord that Scripture records this musing by God: "Shall I hide from Abraham that thing which I do?" (Genesis 18:17).

As a very successful businessman and rancher, Abraham became one of the wealthiest men of his day. When it came to leadership abilities, he was a leader even among his business associates. He stood admirably before his household. He possessed military generalship. It isn't that he never failed; he did so more than once. He was human and not to be excused for his wrongs, but he was also a noble man.

One of Abraham's most admirable qualities was his refusal to run from one of the most difficult experiences of his life. It would be a hard circumstance for anyone: God told Abraham to offer up his son upon a fiery altar of sacrifice. What a difficult divine request! He must have wondered if it really could have come from God at all—especially the Lord who was his friend!

In responding, Abraham had two options: he could have run away from God and what He evidently wanted, he could have taken his family and all he possessed back to Ur; or he could face the difficulty, believing God knew what He was doing and was still Abraham's friend. He chose the second option. He didn't run away (Genesis 22:1-14).

Abraham was probably between 115 and 120 when he faced the most difficult test of his faith. We must learn early in life, and accept it in a healthy way, that we never outgrow problems. Job said, "Yet man is born unto trouble, as the sparks fly upward" (Job 5:7). This well-known sufferer of long ago was right. We can't afford to feel that after we get beyond a certain age, life will be smooth sailing. It is most unrealistic to think that way. God has lessons for us to learn regardless of our age. This learning often comes about via difficulties.

There's another dimension to Abraham's experience which may come as a bit of a surprise. The man was an outstanding believer yet he had that severe difficulty. His life with God was rich. It got better every day. Abraham and God walked together. At times it must have almost been heaven upon earth. In spite of this, the difficulty came. So often it is supposed that becoming a Christian keeps one from difficulty, particularly if one is a good "working-at-it" Christian. But this is not the case, for a life with no problems is not the joy-filled life. God does not keep difficulties from His children. Paul caught the essence of this philosophy and wrote: "And not only so, but we glory in tribulations also: knowing that tribulation worketh patience; and patience, experience; and experience, hope: and hope maketh not ashamed; because the love of God is shed abroad in our hearts by the Holy Ghost which is given unto us" (Romans 5:3-5).

Abraham's difficulty was puzzling from another perspective. His son, Isaac, was the individual through whom God had promised Abraham the world would be blessed. Yet Abraham was asked to sacrifice Isaac. More than this, the father loved his boy especially deeply. The feeling was mutual. In fact, Abraham and Isaac were a team. They walked along in the difficulty together.

Who can even imagine the pain in Abraham's heart? It must have been personal in the keenest way. It must have stirred an inner conflict in his soul such as he had never known before. Every step of those thirty-eight miles to Mt. Moriah must have been as a fresh death for Abraham. Each of the three days they journeyed probably were agony. The Hebrews have a special love for and devotion to their children. Abraham, their father, epitomized it all. God was touching one of Abraham's dearest, most tender spots.

Our difficulties often come at our dearest spots too, where they sting the most. No part of our life is protected just because it is deeply treasured. When God allows difficulty, it isn't that He has a cruel nature but because at that special point our greatest blessing through difficulty can be experienced.

Since Abraham didn't retreat, how did he manage to face the difficulty? Abraham's crucial experience was a test; God was testing His friend. God did not test him hoping the good man would fail, nor because He did not know how Abraham would react. The purpose was to help Abraham see clearly that there wasn't a difficulty in life that he, in company with his Lord, couldn't handle.

This is the basic understanding you must have of your difficulties too. God is testing, not punishing, you. He is not toying with you as though you were a puppet on a string. In your hour of serious testing the consequences are great and the potential for good, exciting. Running away would mean failing the test, with all the remorse and regret such failure brings. But in refusing to run, you will pass the test and enjoy forever the fruits of success.

Too, your success in the test of difficulty may be a tremendous teaching instrument for those who know you and have been watching. Today we who read Abraham's story in the Word of God see in it the love of the Heavenly Father for Jesus, His Son, and the sacrifice He made in order that we might have an opportunity to become sons and daughters of God.

Abraham's difficulty was a test of his love for God. Through it the Lord was saying, "Do you love Me more than anyone else?" By confronting his difficult task Abraham answered a resounding, "Yes!" Often the Lord asks that question of those who claim to follow Him. He asked Peter, "Simon, son of Jonas, lovest thou me more than these?" (John 21:15).

Through your adverse circumstance Jesus may be asking you the same question. Be honest with yourself. Have you permitted someone or something else to take His place in your affections? Love for the Lord must consciously be set ahead of everything else. All other loves must be relegated to their proper places. When this is done, this supreme devotion to God will result in an enriching of the other loves of your life. And your cup will run over. This could be the divine reasoning lying at the core of your present test.

Abraham had absolute, total faith in God. He trusted that God in His perfect wisdom knew what He was doing and that He loved Abraham. He believed God keeps His word no matter how serious the difficulty His child goes through. To Abraham, since the promise of God is unbreakable, His word was worthy of complete trust. In fact, Abraham was convinced that if it were necessary the Lord could and would bring Isaac back from the dead. By this faith Abraham made his way successfully through his testing. Read Genesis 22:5; Hebrews 11:17-19; and after reading Genesis 22:15-18, answer this question especially for your own benefit: Was Abraham's faith in God justified?

Out of his crisis, Abraham developed a special appreciation of God. He indicated that appreciation by naming the place where the crisis occurred

"Jehovah-jireh" (Genesis 22:14), which can be translated, "The Lord sees," or "the Lord will see to it." Throughout the remainder of his life, Abraham no doubt drew strength from the incident. He knew he could make it through any other trials he might face.

If you believe that the Lord looks with the tenderest care upon you in difficulty, you won't run from it. Every Christian has the right to believe this. God's loving awareness is not only an eternal principle you can apply to life's testings; it is a part of His very person. So let Him join you in a positive step ahead into and through difficulty. It may seem odd, but it's the way to joyful living.

Chapter 13

By Going Where God Is Going

Enjoy Living . . .
By Going Where God Is Going

Ours is a travel-conscious world. For the past decade or two, people of almost all nations have crisscrossed the continents. People of all nations are at the beaches; in the bustling cities; riding cable cars; eating in restaurants; buying tickets to the theater. There are the Japanese with cameras; British with ruddy faces; Orientals with shy and courteous demeanor; people from the Continent speaking in diverse languages; women of India in their long, graceful saris; robed Arabs whose homes are in the Middle East; and people of all colors and features dressed in western garb.

Travel has become very big business, for not only does it embrace the tourist; it counts thousands of businessmen among its clients and helps other thousands accomplish glad or sorrowful errands. If you have traveled, you know that the most important thing is not how you travel but where you're going. It's where you're headed that really counts. The bottom line is destination.

In life, too, the direction you've set for yourself is most serious. If you were to ask yourself where you are going, you probably would have many answers. But, above all, the wisest and best answer would be: I am going where God is going. This may sound like a presumptuous reply, yet it is exactly what our Heavenly Father desires of us. God's message to human beings is, "Come, join Me where I'm going and in what I'm doing." Abundant living is based on whether or not you will accept the invitation.

God has created us and the universe and He did it for a purpose. That design is still operative, the disastrous and devastating experience of the human family notwithstanding. Since we have been created with the capacity for such a partnership with God, it is no wonder participation in it fulfills one's life.

It is important that we understand the direction in which God is heading. In our day, and ever since the death and resurrection of Christ, God has been intent on adding to His family. This is plainly stated in Hebrews 2:10: "For it became him, for whom are all things, and by whom are all things, in bringing many sons unto glory, to make the captain of their salvation perfect through sufferings." When we think of the agony Jesus went through when He died on the cross, we can understand the act as the Son of

God making it possible for the Heavenly Father to satisfy His heart's desire to bring millions into His family.

Some of Jesus' last words before returning to heaven included instructions to His followers as to the direction their lives should take. We read in Matthew 28:18-20: "And Jesus came and spake unto them, saying, All power is given unto me in heaven and in earth. Go ye therefore, and teach all nations, baptizing them in the name of the Father, and of the Son, and of the Holy Ghost: Teaching them to observe all things whatsoever I have commanded you: and, lo, I am with you alway, even unto the end of the world. Amen." Luke 24:46,47 states: "And [He] said unto them, Thus it is written, and thus it behoved Christ to suffer, and to rise from the dead the third day: And that repentance and remission of sins should be preached in his name among all nations, beginning at Jerusalem."

If you are going where God is going you will be concerned about people—the whole world. You will be concerned that by faith in Jesus Christ the Saviour they have their sins forgiven, meet God, and be born again entering His eternal family. Do people and their everlasting welfare mean that much to you? Do you care whether or not they have this relationship with God? If you do and you are committed to that goal, you are going where God is going. However, if you are concerned principally with yourself and the accumulation of things, you and God are poles apart. The emphasis God places upon the spiritual family does not mean He is unconcerned about human, physical woes. He is deeply grieved at the problems people have in their lives and in our world. He shows His compassion for the human dilemma by having His children love people in His name, love them so much that they try to heal the wounds and bring new life.

In pointing this out to His disciples, Jesus reminded them: "Ye are the salt of the earth: but if the salt have lost his savour, wherewith shall it be salted? It is thenceforth good for nothing, but to be cast out, and to be trodden under foot of men. Ye are the light of the world. A city that is set on a hill cannot be hid. Neither do men light a candle, and put it under a bushel, but on a candlestick; and it giveth light unto all that are in the house. Let your light so shine before men, that they may see your good works, and glorify your Father which is in heaven" (Matthew 5:13-16).

It is important to understand at this point that going in God's direction is costly. It requires depth of dedication and seriousness of purpose. Whatever the cost, it is worth it because you're going where God is going. Some words of Christ underscore this fact, reminding us this is the way to the truly rich life. "And when he had called the people unto him with his disciples also, he said unto them, Whosoever will come after me, let him deny himself, and take up his cross, and follow me. For whosoever will save his life shall lose it; but whosoever shall lose his life for my sake and the gospel's, the same shall save it" (Mark

8:34,35).

The second point in the direction God is going is this: God is going to send His Son back into this world. Jesus is coming again, first to remove His church from the world and then to return to bring justice to all mankind. He will Himself take the reins of world government into His hands. Ruling from Jerusalem, the Lord Jesus will lead the world into the blessings of living which the Heavenly Father wanted them to have in the first place. The dreams and hopes of the age will become realities. Even nature will sing and rejoice in its recovered beauty and splendor. Among the many Scriptures which tell of this happening, carefully ponder Isaiah 9:6,7; 24:23; Psalm 2; Jeremiah 23:5,6; Daniel 7:13,14; Matthew 2:1,2; Matthew 25:31-33; Luke 1:30-33; John 18:37; Romans 8:21,22; I Corinthians 15:20-26; Philippians 2:9-11; Revelation 11:15; and 19:11-16.

Paul writes: "Having made known unto us the mystery of his will, according to his good pleasure which he hath purposed in himself: That in the dispensation of the fulness of times he might gather together in one all things in Christ, both which are in heaven, and which are on earth; even in him" (Ephesians 1:9,10). One must conclude that God is moving toward the goal of bringing all humanity and every part of creation under the rulership of Jesus Christ. He will rule everything. In going where God is going, look ahead and plan for that time. Be utterly devoted to the Lord Jesus and the biblical Christian cause. To treat this Person with a shrug of the shoulders is to be out of step with God. Some day Christ is going to mean everything to this world.

A man comes to mind who demonstrates how one might take practical steps in going where God is going. He is mentioned briefly in the New Testament and it is entirely possible you have never heard of Epaphras from the city of Colosse. Paul mentions him, almost in passing, but with deep love and respect in Colossians 1:7,8; 4:12,13, and Philemon 23.

Epaphras was committed to helping Christians "stand perfect and complete in all the will of God" (Colossians 4:12). That is simply and surely going where God is going. At some point in time, this man had made a decision to become involved with what God was doing. He gave himself to it no matter what the price in life and energy. It dominated his heart. A person like this may not be distinguished in the world. He may be listed on the back pages of the book of human greatness, or, most likely, he won't be found there at all. But to the Lord and the group to which Epaphras was related, he was prized and precious. And this is where eminence really matters! The question is, in what ways did he make his going where God is going effective?

For starters, Epaphras was convinced of the significance of the church as Christ saw it and as Paul described it. Evidently, to him the most important people in the world were believers in Christ wherever they were, and particularly those in the church in the town where he lived. So he became a part of the church, the body of believers. Paul referred to him as, "one of you" (Colossians 4:12). Jesus established the church as the instrument through which God would do His will in the world. This is what Christ said about the church founded upon the solid rock of His person: "And I say also unto thee, that thou art Peter, and upon this rock I will build my church; and the gates of hell shall not prevail against it" (Matthew 16:18).

What do you think of the Christian church—one that believes as a Christian church should—one that acts as a Christian church should, according to the standards set by the Bible? The Lord sees His church as the most precious body of people in the world because it took the death of His Son to bring it into being. Paul puts God's evaluation of the church into these words, "the church of God, which he hath purchased with his own blood" (Acts 20:28). The same author tells of Jesus' feeling toward the church: "Christ . . . loved the church, and gave himself for it" (Ephesians 5:25).

To go where God is going you must be a part of a Christian church. Trusting its Saviour, Jesus Christ. Participating in its worldwide mission. Supporting it in its valid programs. Defending it against its detractors. Sharing your gifts and talents with the church and its calling. The church, true to Scripture, is where the presence of God is and the base from which He is moving in His first-stage efforts.

In going where God is going Epaphras assumed

the spirit of a servant. He had a desire to help people—not hypocritically but genuinely; not boastfully but honestly. He is called "fellowservant" and "faithful minister" (Colossians 1:7); and again, "A servant of Christ . . . always labouring fervently for you in prayers" (Colossians 4:12). He went in God's direction humbly, diligently and selflessly, glorifying Christ and making Him live for people. Epaphras' attitude was identical to Paul's. Even more meaningfully, it was identical to Christ's.

The spirit in which you go where God is going has much to do with your effectiveness in that work. You cannot truly be a partner with God and at the same time have an attitude of spiritual superiority. Through a ministering spirit, eternal things can be accomplished. "But Jesus called them to him, and saith unto them, Ye know that they which are accounted to rule over the Gentiles exercise lordship over them; and their great ones exercise authority upon them. But so shall it not be among you: but whosoever will be great among you, shall be your minister: and whosoever of you will be the chiefest, shall be servant of all. For even the Son of man came not to be ministered unto, but to minister, and to give his life a ransom for many" (Mark 10:42-45).

Undoubtedly the greatest thing Epaphras did as he joined God in His holy purpose was to pray for the people of the church, that they might really go where God was going. In this he was most conspicuous. Right here he becomes a great example for us to imitate. Epaphras was deeply serious about his praying. He agonized in it. His efforts in prayer were passionate. He strained every nerve and used every resource of his personality.

It takes discipline to pray like this, but you could do nothing more important in your joint efforts with God. Prayer of this caliber is work. It is warfare in the spiritual realm. It is engagement in the supreme contest. It is a warrior standing in the breach against the enemies of God and refusing to budge an inch or to be defeated. This kind of prayer is consistent, constant, purposeful. It is immediate when threats arise or opportunities are presented to gain ground for God. Without prayer of this kind, much of what God wants done remains undone. One of the greatest challenges and responsibilities we face is an earnest prayer life; that is, if we're going where God is going.

Quite possibly in your travel through life you have come to an intersection. From it radiate many different directions you may take. Among them, one marker catches your eye. It reads, "God's Way." On it you recognize signs that Jesus has gone that route. So have Paul, Peter, John, Epaphras and scores of others. There aren't as many people on this road as you see on the others. But you know it's the only highway bringing you to abundant, joy-filled living. You have a serious and far-reaching decision to make. No one can do it for you. Put your life on the right road. Go where God is going!